Ladle, Leaf, & Loaf

EX LIBRIS

Ladle, Leaf, & Loaf

Soup, Salad, and Bread
for Every Season

WRITTEN AND ILLUSTRATED
BY LISA COWDEN

HOUGHTON MIFFLIN COMPANY
BOSTON NEW YORK

For information about permission to reproduce selections from this book, write to Permissions, Houghton Mifflin Company, 215 Park Avenue South, New York, New York 10003.

Visit our Web site: www.hmco.com/trade.

Library of Congress Cataloging-in-Publication Data

Cowden, Lisa.

Ladle, leaf, and loaf: soup, salad, and bread for every season /

written and illustrated by Lisa Cowden.

p.   cm.

Includes index.

ISBN 0-395-96715-5

1. Soups. 2. Salads. 3. Bread. I. Title.

TX757.C69 2000

641.8'13—dc21   00-026915

Book design by Susan McClellan

Printed in the United States of America

QUM 10 9 8 7 6 5 4 3 2

In memory of my father, whose keen powers of observation and the joy he experienced from his insights taught me that this is, truly, a world of wonders.

Acknowledgments

I WOULD LIKE TO THANK MY AGENT, Glen Hartley, for his gracious support and the effort he made on my behalf. It is my good fortune that this book has been in such competent hands at Houghton Mifflin, and to everyone there, I extend my gratitude. In particular, my editor, Rux Martin, deserves my thanks and appreciation for the skill and clarity she brought to the task, as well as for her accessibility and sense of humor. Special thanks to Lori Galvin-Frost for her efficiency, enthusiasm, and good cheer; to Michaela Sullivan for the excellent work she did on the cover; to Susan McClellan for her perceptive rendering of the design of the book, and to my copyeditor, Deborah Kops, for her help in guiding this book to the finish line.

Thanks are also due to my many friends who came for dinner on the condition they would critique the food; to the staff of Now You're Cooking in Ithaca, New York, for their help in answering my questions about utensils and ingredients; and to my daughter, Charlotte, for her insights about this book. But most of all, my heartfelt gratitude to my good friend Paddy Flavelle for reading the manuscript and reminding me to listen to my muses and "let those horses run."

Contents

THE THEME OF SOUP, SALAD, AND BREAD IS SO RICH and varied that Proteus himself would have trouble exhausting the possibilities. The combinations can be as plain or as fancy as you like, and any one of the three can serve as the focal point or inspiration for a meal, starting a creative chain reaction. Chilled Fresh Green Pea Soup garnished with a dollop of Minted Yogurt Cheese would be the perfect partner for French Bread and Chive Butter. Add a Radish and Cucumber Salad with Green Herb Dressing, and Pan might be tempted to show up at the table. A Golden Lemon Chicken Soup accompanied by tender Big Buttermilk Biscuits can ward off the cold when the seasons change and the nights lengthen, and you can add Endive Salad with Roasted Garlic Dressing for a touch of elegance. And so it goes, through innumerable combinations.

I was first introduced to the mix-and-match possibilities of these basic foods many years ago when I worked in a vegetarian restaurant. We ran a somewhat irreverent, slightly raucous kitchen, creating menus based on whatever fresh produce was available from our local buyer and on the contents of our larder, which was supplied by a natural foods company. Between the Italian grocer and the hippies driving semis, we had plenty of material to work with.

My favorite meal was our "cheap eats" dinner in the middle of the week, when we served soup, salad, and bread. We called it "Poor Man's Night"—a lapse in political correctness that wouldn't be tolerated today, although the nutritional correctness of the meals was ahead of its time. Unlike other nights, when we followed a standard repertoire, there was no end to the variety of the dishes we came up with for Poor Man's Night. I made many huge pots of soup, jars of salad dressing, and loaves of bread during my shifts and never tired of the challenge of coming up with something new. Since I left the restaurant, I've stopped dancing to Crosby, Stills, Nash and Young when I cook, but I've continued to explore the culinary possibilities of creating meals built on the simple foundation of ladle, leaf, and loaf.

Warm soups that feature a vegetable form a large, congenial group, quite different in character from the implied elegance of chilled soups in this volume. Homestyle breads have their own comfortable niche, apart from suave French bread. The same diversity shows up in the salad section, which ranges from a simple bowl of leaves with a splash of dressing to salads with such panache, they can only be called Dazzlers.

Condiments, dressings, and spreads highlight the flavors of soup, salad, or bread and lend an aesthetic flair to this unassuming trio. While the recipe partnerships in these pages reflect my sensibilities, they're only suggestions, meant to invite you to put on your apron and have some fun.

The creative process bears a more than passing resemblance to the way we go about ordinary tasks, and I've found that the differences between the studio and the kitchen are not as great as I'd imagined. A blank page, an empty soup pot, a dormant salad bowl, an idle bread board, and art supplies in repose on the studio table all represent the same creative challenge: to bring inspiration to fruition.

Ingredients

WE COOKS ARE AN OPINIONATED BUNCH—micromanagers all. Someone figured that out long ago, saddling us with that business about spoiling the broth. But it turns out that it's not such a bad thing to develop strong preferences for specific ingredients. The contents of the pantry are much the same as a painter's palette; they reflect each cook's unique approach to food through the choices we make at the grocery store and market.

What follows is my palette—a general list of the ingredients that appear

throughout this book, with comments on some of their quirks and virtues as I've come to know them.

Regardless of what you select from this repertoire, remember that the hub, the core, the quintessence of good cooking is using the freshest ingredients of the best quality you can afford. With the exception of a few indulgences, the recipes in this book call for ingredients that are readily available and reasonably priced.

Buttermilk: The chemistry between leavening agents and buttermilk adds a lovely flavor and moisture to quick breads.

Canned Broth: An alternative to making soup stock from scratch. Just remember that you will have to decrease the amount of salt in a recipe if you use canned broth, which is already salted.

Chicken: Finding good chicken can be a challenge. By "good chicken" I mean birds that are as fresh and unadulterated as possible, without unpleasant amounts of excess fat, and as far before the expiration date as possible. It's best to cook chicken the day it is purchased; and remember that the recommended refrigerator shelf life of cooked chicken and chicken broth is three days.

Chili, canned, dried, and ground: For some reason I haven't figured out, whole canned green chilies are superior in flavor and texture to the chopped variety. When it comes to dried chilies, whole or ground, the best I've found are from Chimayo, New Mexico; the flavor is consistent and evocative. You can order Chimayo chilies from The Chile Shop: 109 East Water Street, Santa Fe, New Mexico 87501. Phone (505) 983-6080.

Citrus rind, grated: Wash that lemon or orange well before grating! I suspect that unless you pick them off your own trees, whatever you wash off is something you'd rather not eat.

Cornmeal: Lots to choose from, and the variations make a difference in how moist, chewy, and corn-flavored your breads will be. The finer cornmeals tend to make drier, lighter breads, whereas loaves made from more coarsely ground meal have a denser texture.

Dashi tea bags: These ingenious "tea bags" make a fine fish-flavored broth that is the standard base for miso soup. They can also be used in seafood soups instead of homemade fish stock. Look for them in the Japanese food section of the grocery store or in a Japanese market.

Flour: Bread flour and chickpea flour can be found in a health food store. The garden-variety all-purpose flour from the grocery store is an acceptable substitute for bread flour, although I think bread flour is superior. It has more gluten and protein and improves the texture and flavor of homemade breads.

Garlic: A staple item and the godfather of the larder, whose presence you shouldn't ignore. Check periodically to see that your supply is fresh: You can't get much flavor from garlic that has started to dry out. Select firm bulbs and store them in a cool, dry spot, and your garlic should keep for two to three weeks.

Herbs, fresh or dried: the adjectives of cooking. Dried herbs gradually lose their potency and should be tested occasionally for flavor and aroma. Some herbs, such as parsley, cilantro, and chervil, are better fresh; they smell and taste like grass clippings when dried. Other herbs, such as basil, tarragon, sage, and thyme, make the transition from fresh to dried without losing their character.

Miso: Think of miso as a bouillon cube in a slightly different form. A dollop of miso in soup may be just what you need to develop the flavor of the broth. There are many kinds of miso, varying in color from light to dark; in general, lighter misos are milder, and darker misos have a stronger flavor. Miso can be found in health food stores.

Neufchâtel cheese: One of those familiar foods with unrecognized potential. I like having it on hand because it's easy to whip up interesting and unusual low-fat spreads using it as a base.

Nuts: Ground nuts add moisture and flavor to baked goods, and toasted nuts make excellent condiments. Toasting enhances their flavors and gives them a nice crunchy texture. Instructions for toasting nuts are on page 38. As a garnish for soups, nuts provide an interesting and contrasting texture and an unusual visual accent.

Oil: Olive, canola, peanut, sesame, and walnut—my favorites in descending order of preference. I use olive and canola most frequently because of their nutritional value, versatility, and flavor. Peanut, sesame, and walnut oil have distinctive flavors that are appropriate for certain dishes.

Onions: A larder without onions means it's time to go to the grocery store. Once you get there, before you toss a bag of the familiar yellow onions into your cart, consider trying some of the other varieties, such as Vidalia sweets or red onion.

Peppercorns: Aside from being quite beautiful to look at (they get big points from me in this department), black and green peppercorns will give your dishes plenty of heat. Pink peppercorns have an astonishing flavor: Slightly sweet, spicy, and warm, they are not as hot and are far more subtle than other peppercorns.

Salt: I prefer kosher salt instead of table salt for aesthetic and practical reasons. Compared with table salt, an equal amount of kosher salt tastes less salty, and I find it easier to use when adjusting the seasonings of a dish.

Seafood: If you can (1) find out when the seafood is delivered to your grocery store, (2) be there the day it arrives, (3) cook your "catch" before the sun rises the next day, and (4) refrain from overcooking it, you've mastered the ideal strategy for cooking fish.

Seaweed: These vegetables from the sea come in many "forms," textures, and subtle flavors. The recipes in this book that call for dried seaweed provide instructions for reconstituting it by soaking it in water. Seaweed can be found in health food stores, Asian markets, or the Asian food section of the grocery store.

Seeds: If you buy organic seeds, some vigilance is required when storing them. It's been my experience that sesame and poppy seeds stay fresher if they are refrigerated because of their oil content. Furthermore, some critters find organic food very attractive, and refrigeration is a great deterrent to them, particularly my least favorite uninvited guest: the food moth. The food moth eats indiscriminately, sampling not only seeds, but grains and flours as well. Highly processed food, or "chem food," as it's known in some circles, is a less likely target for bugs, but no wonder—it has less food value! I'll take "real food" any day, and risk sharing it with a random bug.

Soup bones: The best soup bones are the ones the butcher cuts for you while you wait. I'm a stickler for freshness when it comes to meats. If finding a freshly cut soup bone isn't an option and I have to choose packaged meat, I pay close attention to the expiration date and look for a fresh color.

Spices: If your dried spices fail to pass the sniff-and-taste test, they are ghosts of their former selves. Time for a fresh supply!

Sun-dried tomatoes: Aside from seaweed, sun-dried tomatoes are the best "just add water" vegetables around. Their concentrated flavor and meaty texture add a lot of character to soup.

Tamari: Tamari is naturally brewed soy sauce made entirely from soybeans. It has a smoother taste and more flavor than regular soy sauce. Tamari can be purchased in health food stores, Japanese grocery stores, and the international food section of most supermarkets.

Vegetables: Choose those that still have moisture, crispness, and firmness—indications that their life force hasn't abandoned them entirely.

Vinegar: Regular and white balsamic, red and white wine, rice wine, and raspberry are among my favorites. Cider and herb vinegars are also good to have on hand. These are all available in most supermarkets.

Yogurt: Plain nonfat yogurt is excellent for condiments, spreads, and salad dressings. Drained nonfat yogurt (called yogurt cheese; see page 41) is a very good low-fat substitute for sour cream.

Menus

MENU SUGGESTIONS, taken at face value, can be very helpful. It's like being given a good map from AAA with your route highlighted in yellow marker: You end up with a meal and bypass the problem of coming up with dishes that complement one another. This is good news for the novice; furthermore, a well-orchestrated menu teaches a lot about cooking. It's a condensed lesson in learning to balance flavors and combine ingredients and can be an introduction to a new point of view.

For more experienced cooks, following a menu becomes an information-gathering mission. It's an opportunity to explore someone else's sensibilities and opinions. You can get a lot of mileage and inspiration out of cruising cookbooks, reading menus, and sorting through other people's culinary psyches.

We've all had occasions, however, when reading a map is not as much of an adventure as striking out on your own. In that spirit, consider these menus as suggestions—ideas to stimulate your culinary imagination, whet your appetite, and get the creative juices flowing.

~ Spring ~

Asparagus Essence with Toasted Almonds (page 37) . . . Wild Rice Salad
with Walnut Oil and Lemon Dressing (page 177) . . . Saffron Rolls (page 191)
with Chive Butter (page 247)

Spinach and Onion Soup with Rosemary Walnut Dumplings (page 44) . . .
Cucumber Salad with Creamy Garlic Dressing (page 136) . . .
Whole Wheat Soda Bread (page 229)

Saffron Salmon Chowder with Sweet Peppers (page 110) . . . Mixed Green
Salad with Red Wine Vinegar Dressing (page 180) . . . Spiral Herb Bread
(page 206) with Chive Butter (page 247)

~ Summer ~

Chilled Zucchini and Carrot Soup (page 90) . . . Chicken Salad with Caper Dressing (page 165) . . . French Bread (page 198) with Pesto Cheese Spread (page 254)

Gazpacho with Fresh Tarragon (page 89) . . . Tabbouleh Salad with Feta Dressing (page 115) . . . Onion Flatbread (page 212) with Sun-Dried Tomato Tapenade (page 252)

Pureed Corn Soup with Avocado (page 47) . . . Fresh Pepper Salad with Basil Dressing (page 168) . . . Savory Zucchini Bread (page 233) with Parmesan Cheese Spread (page 253)

~ Autumn ~

Red and Yellow Tomato Soup with Broiled Tomatoes (page 50) . . . Shrimp Salad with Wilted Lettuce and Balsamic Vinaigrette (page 133) . . . Forty-Clove Garlic Bread (page 196)

Roasted Red Pepper Soup with Crisp Julienned Potatoes (page 53) . . . Summer Garden Salad with Tarragon Vinaigrette (page 177) and Herb and Cheese Croutons (page 67) . . . Cornmeal Popovers (page 222) with Lemon Honey Butter (page 245)

Pureed Fennel Soup with Steamed Julienned Carrots and Toasted Walnuts (page 70) . . . Root Vegetable Slaw with Creamy Caraway Dressing (page 148) . . . Potato-Onion Rye Bread (page 202)

~ Winter ~

Potato-Kale Soup with Toasted Walnuts (page 64) . . . Beet Salad with Capers and Pickled Onions (page 146) . . . Crusty Whole Wheat Bread (page 199) with Anchovy Butter (page 250)

Golden Lemon Chicken Soup with Egg Noodles (page 102) . . . Endive Salad with Roasted Garlic Dressing (page 175) . . . Big Buttermilk Biscuits (page 242)

Portobello Mushroom and Barley Soup with Garlic Croutons (page 78) . . . English Cucumber and Onion Salad with Buttermilk Dressing (page 137) . . . Garlic Breadsticks (page 189)

Sizing It Up

WHEN IT COMES TO MEASURING ingredients, baking is a snap. Leveling a cup of flour with a knife guarantees accuracy. A "large" egg is, well, a large egg, clearly not "small" or "jumbo." Things are not as obvious when making soups and salads. What, for example, is a "small" onion? How can you tell what "4 medium-sized red-skinned potatoes" really means? How big is a "large" clove of garlic?

As I worked on the recipes for this book, I even considered including some kind of guide for vegetable sizes. But that seemed a bit much and reminiscent of one of those ultra-fastidious gadgets to measure spaghetti, which I never, ever, use. "Why all the angst?" one might ask. I suppose it's because having a good meal is like hearing live music. Each performance happens only once, and if it's a good one, it bears repeating. Of course, the next time it will be different, but a close approximation or even a better rendition is always a possibility!

In keeping with the hope that these recipes will be a point of departure for many a good meal, I have tried to be specific about ingredients without going overboard.

Utensils

FOR EVERY POT, THERE'S A LID, as the saying goes. That's a reassuring sentiment when it refers to romance, and it could have been coined by a cook with either a well-appointed kitchen or the ability to wing it. Most of us fall somewhere in between the boundaries of owning pot racks festooned with glowing utensils and using a wine bottle as a rolling pin, and we manage well enough. I have no advice to offer the lovelorn, but I do have some suggestions regarding cooking equipment. When it comes to tools, the ones that make the job easier and more efficient are worth having on hand. It turns out that innate practicality is also quite attractive. Who says you can't develop a romance with your pots and pans?

What follows is hardly an exhaustive inventory of kitchen utensils and equipment. Instead, this list highlights some of the items I have found particularly useful for making soups, salads, and breads.

Baking sheets and loaf pans: I prefer heavy-gauge 13-x-18-inch baking sheets and standard 8½-x-4½-inch loaf pans. The loaf pans get a good rinse with hot soapy water, but I refrain from vigorous scrubbing; a well-seasoned pan bakes better crusts.

Bowls: I use an assortment of stainless steel and ceramic mixing bowls, with at least one wide-bottomed bowl among them. These are great for mixing bread before moving the dough to a floured surface.

Cutting boards: Having several of varying sizes can give you a lot of extra surface area for cutting, chopping, and even kneading. Using separate cutting boards for meats and produce can help keep your foods from becoming contaminated by bacteria. Plastic cutting boards, which can be put in the dishwasher or scrubbed with hot soapy water, are better for meats. Either plastic or wooden cutting boards can be used for vegetables and fruits and should be washed thoroughly.

Foley food mill: It looks something like a pot with a built-in strainer and paddle. Placed over a bowl, it separates the seeds and skins of fruits and vegetables as they are pureed. This indispensable member of the old guard is the hand version of food processors and blenders.

Food processors: Better than a blender, they are easier to use and clean, and they have more attachments. For small portions and for grinding nuts and seeds, use a mini, 2-cup capacity food processor.

Garlic peeler and garlic press: Someone was really thinking when she came up with this little gadget, a rubber tube five inches long and an inch wide that makes peeling garlic ridiculously easy. Just pop a clove in the tube, roll it back and forth on a hard surface, give it a shake, and out comes a whole, peeled clove of garlic! If you can find a garlic press that comes apart so that it can be cleaned easily, don't let it out of your sight. It is most likely to be French.

Gravy separator: Another item that deserves high praise, a gravy separator is a small measuring cup with a spout near the bottom. When the cup is filled with stock, the fat rises to the top, enabling the cook to pour out the stock without the fat. It's much faster than chilling the stock and removing the layer of fat.

Knives: The old rule holds true: Keep your knives sharp and buy the type that can be sharpened with a stone. Paring knives, a small chef's knife, a cleaver, and a carving knife are my personal favorites; you ought to be able to cover all the bases with these.

Mortar and pestle: Often ignored because they seem to have their limitations. Not so! They can pulverize with the best of them, and there's nothing better for crushing peppercorns.

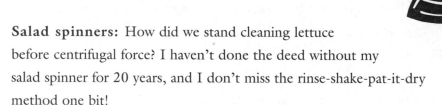

Rubber spatulas: Seems that one can't have too many, especially the thinner kind.

Salad spinners: How did we stand cleaning lettuce before centrifugal force? I haven't done the deed without my salad spinner for 20 years, and I don't miss the rinse-shake-pat-it-dry method one bit!

Sieve: A very fine sieve is the utensil of choice for making yogurt cheese, herb butters, and fine-textured soups.

Soup bowls: Wide and shallow, for the best presentation. Individual pasta bowls are great for this job and are also excellent for serving salads.

Stockpot, soup pot: Both essential. I use a (tall, thin, good-looking) 2-gallon stockpot and a 4½-quart soup pot. Stainless steel is best.

Whisk: The only tool I use when blending puree into stock. I gave up on wire whisks, aesthetic though they are, and bought a stainless steel one with a solid handle from a restaurant supply store. It's a bit more pliable than the wire versions, and it won't rust!

Soup

I'VE ALWAYS FELT A KINSHIP WITH THE SOLDIER-turned-chef in the folk tale who started with a pot of water and a stone and ended up with soup. He used basic kitchen chemistry and made it seem like magic with a little sleight of hand: The universal solvent (water) plus the powers of persuasion (the odd potato, carrot, and herbs coaxed from the unsuspecting villagers) equals soup. This is a good formula to remember; it's food for the table and food for thought.

Like the soldier in the folk tale, I used to make soup by adding vegetables to a pot of water, but I've learned that it's a far less random experience to start with the vegetables. My soups have a theme now, and this strategy has gotten me past the problems I used to encounter trying to throw things together and hoping for the best after a raid on the contents of the larder and the refrigerator. And as for the many times I still peer into the refrigerator as though I am consulting an oracle, I owe thanks to the aforementioned storybook character for helping me see the contents as a source of inspiration instead of a reservoir of good intentions.

Soup is the original comfort food and the universal one-dish meal. It covers all the bases: something to eat, something to drink, and even something to cure what ails you—if the dish happens to be chicken soup. I've even eaten soup for breakfast and can vouch for its power to sustain the body and soul for the better part of a day. So listen up, Mock Turtle, soup is a beautiful thing at any time, not just in the evening.

Ladle, Leaf, & Loaf

GOOD STOCK" can refer to a prize herd of cattle, a nice portfolio, or a pot of carefully made broth. They all have one thing in common: There's a pretty good chance they bring a good return on the investment. When it comes to soup, a good stock can make the difference between "dinner" and "a dining experience."

There is an ongoing debate between the traditionalists and the advocates of convenience regarding stocks. The purists argue that

making stock from scratch is superior because the ingredients are fresh, while the opportunists point out that making stock can be time-consuming. I consider it a lesson in understanding where food really comes from.

For the same reason, I used to raise my own chickens. After several years of trying the philosophy of "if you eat meat, then grow your own," which included slaughtering and butchering the birds, finding a local chicken slaughterhouse was a blessing. I discovered the convenience of taking a crate of squawking birds there in the morning and picking up a box of freshly butchered chickens on ice that afternoon, looking just like what I could buy in the grocery store. Of course it dawned on me that I was going about things the hard way, and so ended my chicken career.

Never making a soup stock from scratch, though, is taking a detour past the basic principles of cooking. In hindsight, I could have taken a detour when it came to chickens, but I'm very glad I don't do so with soup.

To give the other side of the debate its due, though, there are occasions when canned stock is perfectly acceptable and saves you valuable time. Just be aware of its salt content, and experiment to find brands that suit your taste.

Ladle, Leaf, & Loaf

Chicken Stock

MY JEWISH GRANDMOTHER would have approved of this rich stock.
The secret to success is cooking it slowly to reduce the liquid and intensify the flavor.

1 whole 4–5-pound chicken
2½ quarts water
1 small yellow onion, studded
  with 10 cloves
4 sprigs fresh parsley
3 garlic cloves
6 black peppercorns
1 teaspoon kosher salt

Rinse the chicken and remove the excess fat. Put it in a stockpot and cover with the water. Add the remaining ingredients and bring to a boil. Spoon off the scum. Reduce the heat to low and simmer, uncovered, for about 2 hours.

Strain the stock. Degrease with a gravy separator or by chilling the stock and then lifting off the fat. The stock keeps refrigerated for 3 days.

Makes about 1½ quarts

Beef Stock

THERE'S A LITTLE CULINARY MAGIC going on here: This combination of vegetables, herbs, spices, and a good fresh soup bone produces a stock with a lot of character, considering the unassuming nature of the ingredients.

1½ pound beef soup bone with
    meat attached, trimmed of fat

2½ quarts water

1 small yellow onion, studded
    with 5 cloves

1 large carrot, sliced

¼ cup celery leaves

¼ cup fresh parsley leaves

6 black peppercorns

1 bay leaf

1 ¼–1 ½ teaspoons kosher salt,
    or to taste

¼ teaspoon dried thyme

Combine all the ingredients in a stockpot. Bring to a boil and spoon off the scum. Reduce the heat to low and simmer, uncovered, for about 1½ hours. Strain the stock; discard the vegetables. Trim the meat off the bone, if desired. Degrease with a gravy separator or by chilling the stock and lifting off the fat. The stock keeps refrigerated for 3 days.

Makes about 1½ quarts

Fish Stock

THIS IS THE REAL THING, starting from scratch with a fish—minus the fillets.
Once you have the ingredients in the pot, you are just minutes away from a savory stock
that will make a qualitative difference in your fish soups.

**Head, bones, and skin of 2½–3
   pounds fresh fish**
2 **quarts water**
1 **small yellow onion, studded
   with 5 cloves**
⅓ **cup fresh parsley leaves**
4 **celery tops, with leaves**
3 **sprigs fresh savory**
6 **black peppercorns**
1 **bay leaf**
½ **teaspoon kosher salt**

Combine all the ingredients in a stockpot.
Bring to a boil and spoon off the scum. Reduce
the heat to low and simmer, covered, for 20 minutes. Strain the stock. It keeps refrigerated for 3
days.

Makes about 1¾ quarts

Ladle, Leaf, & Loaf

Vegetable Consommé

Vegetable consommé is tricky; to end up with more than salty hot water with a vague reference to vegetables, the ratio of the ingredients is crucial. The idea is to pack those veggies in; they contain a lot of water that helps flavor the broth.

---

1 tablespoon olive oil

1 large yellow onion, quartered and sliced

1 medium leek with some of the green parts, cut in half lengthwise and sliced

4 garlic cloves, sliced

2 cups chopped celery stalks and leaves

2 cups russet potato skins (5–6 medium)

1½ cups chopped kale

2 small carrots, sliced

¼ cup loosely packed fresh parsley leaves

3 fresh basil leaves

1 sprig fresh oregano

1¼ teaspoons kosher salt

Freshly ground black pepper

Pinch of nutmeg

Pinch of paprika

1 ¼-inch-square piece of dried red chili

1½ quarts water

Heat the oil in a stockpot. Add the onion, leek, and garlic, stirring to coat with the oil. Cover and cook over low heat for 3 to 4 minutes. Stir in the remaining vegetables and seasonings. Cover and cook until the vegetables can be pierced with a fork. Add the water. Bring to a boil, cover, and reduce the heat to low. Continue cooking for about 1 hour. Strain the liquid; discard the vegetables. The consommé keeps refrigerated for 3 days.

Makes about 1 quart

Soups that Feature Vegetables

YOU CAN COOK YOUR WAY through the seasons following these recipes, beginning with Asparagus Essence with Toasted Almonds in early spring and ending with hearty Winter Vegetable Soup when it's cold outside and the days are short. Making soup is a nice way to keep your finger on the pulse of the natural world.

Asparagus Essence
with Toasted Almonds

IF YOU WANT to capture the essence of fresh asparagus in the soup pot,
this recipe will do the trick. It's a deliciously persuasive argument
for the merits of simplicity in the kitchen.

3   **pounds fresh asparagus, washed and
    snapped into 1-inch pieces**
1   **tablespoon olive oil**
1   **Vidalia onion, sliced**
2   **cups water**
1   **cup reduced-fat milk or half-and-half
    Kosher salt to taste**

Toasted almonds (page 38)
Chopped fresh chives

Set aside about 18 asparagus tips, cover with plastic wrap, and refrigerate. Heat the oil in a 4½-quart soup pot. Add the onion, stirring to coat with the oil. Cover and cook over medium heat until the onion starts to soften, 3 to 4 minutes. Add the remaining asparagus and stir. Cover and cook for 3 to 4 more minutes.

Add the water. Bring to a boil; reduce the heat to low. Cover and continue cooking until the asparagus can be pierced with a fork, about 20 minutes.

Strain the soup, reserving the vegetables, and return the liquid to the pot. Puree the vegetables in a food processor. Force the puree through a sieve or a Foley food mill. Stir the pureed vegetables into the liquid.

Meanwhile, coat a skillet with vegetable spray. Cook the reserved asparagus tips over medium heat until they begin to turn bright green. Add them to the soup, and stir in the milk or half-and-half until just blended. Reheat gently. Garnish with a sprinkling of the toasted almonds and chopped fresh chives and serve.

Serves 4–6

~ Toasted Nuts and Seeds ~

Toasting nuts and seeds brings their flavors into focus and crisps them up. They make excellent condiments in soup and salads, adding taste and texture and that much-sought-after "finishing touch."

½–2 cups almonds, walnuts, pine nuts, hazelnuts,
sesame seeds, or pumpkin seeds

Preheat the oven to 400 degrees. Spread the nuts or seeds on a baking sheet. Bake for 5 to 8 minutes, shaking the tray occasionally. Cool the nuts or seeds on the baking sheet and store in a tightly lidded container.

Makes 1½–2 cups

Swiss Chard Soup with Miso and Orzo

ORZO AND TOMATOES are juxtaposed with Asian ingredients here.
This is a case where the food definitely tastes as good as it looks.

---

1 tablespoon canola oil

1 large yellow onion, coarsely chopped

1 large garlic clove, sliced

2 tablespoons miso paste

4 cups water

1 pound red or white chard leaves and stems, coarsely chopped

1–2 teaspoons tamari, to taste

1 cup cooked orzo

1½ cups coarsely chopped plum tomatoes (3–4 large)

Slivers of candied ginger

Heat the oil in a 4½-quart soup pot. Add the onion and garlic, stirring to coat with the oil. Cover and cook over medium heat until the vegetables start to soften, 3 to 4 minutes. Meanwhile, in a small bowl, mix the miso paste in 1 cup of the water, stirring to dissolve. Add the miso to the soup pot with the chard, tamari, and the remaining 3 cups water. Cover and cook until the chard wilts, about 5 minutes. Stir in the orzo and add more tamari if necessary. Stir in the tomatoes and heat briefly. Serve the soup garnished with the slivers of candied ginger.

Serves 4

Minted Spinach Soup
with Yogurt Cheese and Toasted Pine Nuts

ONE OF THOSE QUIET LITTLE CULINARY TRICKS shows up in this recipe—pureed cooked white rice. It can thicken soup and make it creamy, is a healthful alternative to milk products, and doesn't mask the flavors of the other ingredients.

½ cup uncooked white rice

5 cups Chicken Stock (page 32)
    or canned broth

1 pound fresh spinach, washed and
    trimmed

¼ teaspoon kosher salt

4–5 fresh mint leaves

Plain Yogurt Cheese (opposite)
    or sour cream
Toasted pine nuts (page 15),
    optional

In a small saucepan, cook the rice in 1 cup of the chicken stock. Set aside. Meanwhile, in a 4½-quart soup pot, combine the remaining 4 cups of stock with the spinach and salt. Cover and cook over medium heat until the spinach wilts. Stir in the mint leaves, cover, and cook for several minutes. Remove from the heat.

Stir the cooked rice into the soup. Puree in a food processor and force the mixture through a sieve. Reheat the soup. Serve, garnished with a dollop of yogurt cheese or sour cream and a sprinkling of the toasted pine nuts, if desired.

Serves 4–6

~ Plain Yogurt Cheese ~

Easy to make, yogurt cheese is the perfect medium for condiments and spreads. Any plain nonfat yogurt will work, but the better the yogurt, the better the cheese.

1 quart nonfat yogurt

Use a sieve with a very fine mesh, or line a colander with paper towels. Suspend the sieve or colander over a medium bowl. Spoon the yogurt into the sieve. Cover with plastic wrap, refrigerate, and allow the whey to drain from the yogurt for a minimum of 5 hours. The cheese is done when it has been reduced in volume by half. It keeps refrigerated for 1 week.

Makes about 2 cups

NEUFCHÂTEL & NONFAT YOGURT

STARTING WITH GOOD MATERIALS is no less important for the cook than the artist. I once taught an art class for preschool children where this lesson was obvious even to the very young. I began with the basics: how to distinguish between average and high-quality art supplies. It didn't take the children long to appreciate the difference between watercolor on newsprint and watercolor on rag paper. Inspiration deserves all the support it can get, and I, for one, am in favor of the best materials available—whether rag paper and sable brushes in the studio or Neufchâtel cheese and good nonfat yogurt in the kitchen. When it comes to making spreads and condiments, these dairy products are the Cinderellas of the larder, ready to be dressed up and transformed into something that exceeds their modest natures.

Plain Neufchâtel cheese on a bagel is one thing, but bring on the crushed red peppercorns or grated lemon peel, garlic, and herbs, and you have a spread with character. The creamy texture and slight tang

of Neufchâtel is the perfect medium for both savory and sweet flavors and can be steered in either direction with appetizing results.

Plain nonfat yogurt begins with a much lower profile than Neufchâtel, bereft of even a hint of elegance in its name. However, the mere act of making nonfat yogurt into yogurt cheese creates some excitement in the kitchen: a sour cream substitute that doesn't have a bevy of undesirable additives and is still reduced in fat! Blended with herbs and spices, yogurt cheese becomes a versatile condiment for soups and can also be used as a spread.

I have experimented with these cheeses with great success, and encourage you to sample the results and try your hand at creating your own recipes.

Spinach and Onion Soup
with Rosemary Walnut Dumplings

Serve THIS soup in wide, shallow bowls to allow plenty of room for the large dumplings.

1 tablespoon olive oil

2 large Vidalia onions, sliced

1 large leek with some of the
   green part, sliced

1 large garlic clove

1¼ pounds fresh spinach, washed
   and trimmed

4 cups Vegetable Consommé (page 35)
   or canned vegetable broth

¾ teaspoon kosher salt

1 1-inch sprig fresh rosemary

Rosemary Walnut Dumplings
  (opposite)
Sour cream

Heat the oil over medium heat in a 4½-quart soup pot. Add the onions, leek, and garlic, stirring to coat with the oil. Cook, covered, until the onion starts to soften, 3 to 4 minutes. Add the spinach, cover, and continue to cook until it wilts, 3 to 4 minutes. Add the consommé or canned broth. Bring to a boil and reduce the heat to low. Stir in the salt, add the rosemary, cover, and simmer for 20 minutes.

Remove from the heat. Strain the soup, reserving the vegetables, and pour the liquid back into the pot. Puree the vegetables in a food processor. Blend the puree into the liquid and reheat the soup.

Cook the dumplings separately. Add 2 or 3 to each bowl just before serving. Garnish with a dollop of the sour cream.

Serves 4–6

Ladle, Leaf, & Loaf

~ Rosemary Walnut Dumplings ~

No matter how often I make them, I'm always amazed by the transformation from dough into dumplings. Light and savory, Rosemary Walnut Dumplings can also be served with Chicken Stock (page 32), Golden Lemon Chicken Soup (page 102), or Herbed Butternut Squash Soup (page 56).

- 1   cup all-purpose flour
- 2   teaspoons baking powder
- ¾   teaspoon finely ground walnuts
- ¼   teaspoon kosher salt
- ¼   teaspoon minced fresh rosemary
- 1   tablespoon chilled unsalted butter
- 1   large egg
- 3   tablespoons skim milk

In a medium bowl, combine the flour, baking powder, walnuts, salt, and rosemary. Blend in the butter, using your fingers. Beat the egg with the milk and pour into the dry ingredients. Stir to form a stiff dough.

Transfer the dough to a lightly floured surface. Roll into a log about 1½ inches thick and 10 inches long. Cut into 8 or 12 pieces and roll each one into a ball. Drop the dumplings into 6 cups boiling water and cook for 10 minutes. Transfer the dumplings to the soup with a slotted spoon.

Makes 8 large or 12 medium dumplings

Zucchini-Potato Soup

I THINK ZUCCHINI have a finite amount of flavor and tenderness—
which is why this recipe calls for only young squash. The larger they grow, the
harder it is for the zucchini to deliver good taste and texture to a dish; it's all over
for the ones lurking in the garden on the way to becoming baseball bats!

---

2 tablespoons olive oil

2 garlic cloves, sliced

1 medium yellow onion, sliced

½ teaspoon minced fresh oregano

5 cups sliced small, tender zucchini
   (3–4 whole), plus 1 cup grated zucchini

1 cup peeled and cubed white-skinned
   potato

3 cups water

Kosher salt and freshly ground black
   pepper to taste

Freshly grated Parmesan cheese
Minced fresh chives

Heat the oil in a 4½-quart soup pot. Stir in the garlic, onion, and oregano, coating them with the oil. Cover and cook over medium heat until softened, 3 to 4 minutes. Stir in the sliced zucchini and potato. Add the water and bring the soup to a boil. Reduce the heat to low and simmer until the vegetables are tender, about 15 minutes.

Strain the soup, reserving the vegetables, and return the liquid to the pot. Puree the vegetables in a food processor, and force the puree through a sieve. Stir the vegetables into the liquid. Add the grated zucchini and salt and pepper. Reheat the soup. Serve with a sprinkling of the Parmesan and chives. The soup can also be chilled before serving.

Serves 6

Ladle, Leaf, & Loaf

Pureed Corn Soup with Avocado

THIS SOUP IS A LITTLE FORAY into the flavors I love from growing up in the Southwest. Pink peppercorns are the perfect accent—an adult addition to my culinary repertoire. I doubt I ever ate one in New Mexico as a kid!

4 cups fresh corn kernels (8–9 ears)

2 cups skim milk

1 tablespoon canola oil

1 large yellow onion, quartered and sliced

1 teaspoon minced fresh oregano or ½ teaspoon dried

1 teaspoon chili powder

1 tablespoon butter

1 tablespoon all-purpose flour

2 cups Chicken Stock (page 32) or canned broth

¼ teaspoon kosher salt

8–12 slices avocado

1–1½ teaspoons crushed pink peppercorns

Steam the corn kernels until tender, about 5 minutes. In a medium saucepan, combine the corn and milk and cook, uncovered, over low heat until the mixture starts to thicken, about 20 minutes. Meanwhile, heat the oil in a small skillet. Add the onion and oregano, stirring to coat with the oil. Sprinkle the chili powder over the onion and cook until the onion starts to soften, 3 to 4 minutes. Stir the onion mixture into the corn. Puree in a food processor; set aside.

Melt the butter over medium heat in a 4½-quart soup pot. Stir in the flour with a whisk to make a smooth paste. Slowly add the chicken stock, stirring constantly. Add the corn puree and blend well. Stir in the salt and cook, uncovered, over medium heat for 20 minutes. Garnish each serving with the avocado slices and a sprinkling of the crushed pink peppercorns.

Serves 4–6

Carrot Soup with Vidalia Onion and Sesame

THE SWEET AND MELLOW FLAVOR of carrots in this soup gets just the slightest bit of salty warmth from the Sesame Condiment—and what a color it is!

1 tablespoon canola oil

2 cups thinly sliced Vidalia onion

1 garlic clove, thinly sliced

5 cups grated carrots (3–4 large)

2 medium red-skinned potatoes, peeled and cut into 1-inch cubes

6 cups Vegetable Consommé (page 35) or canned vegetable broth

¼ cup chopped fresh parsley

Sesame Condiment (opposite)

Heat the oil in a 4½-quart soup pot. Add the onion and garlic, stirring to coat with the oil. Cover and cook over low heat until softened, 3 to 4 minutes. Add the carrots, potatoes, and the consommé or canned broth. Cook, uncovered, over low heat for 30 minutes, or until the vegetables can be pierced with a fork.

Puree the soup in a food processor in small batches. Return the soup to the pot, stir in the parsley, and reheat briefly. Garnish each serving with a sprinkling of the sesame condiment.

Serves 6

~ Sesame Condiment ~

A little goes a long way with this traditional macrobiotic condiment. The addition of dried chives lends a touch of color and flavor that tone down the intensity of this deliberately salty seasoning. It can be used as a salt substitute and to add flavor to salad dressings and spreads.

¼   cup sesame seeds, toasted (page 38)
2½ teaspoons dried chives
½   teaspoon coarse sea salt

Combine the ingredients in a mortar and crush with a pestle until well blended. Store in a small, tightly lidded jar. The condiment keeps about 1 month.

Makes about ⅓ cup

Red and Yellow Tomato Soup
with Broiled Tomatoes

HAVE A LOT OF TOMATOES and not a lot of time before dinner?
You can prepare and serve this soup in about thirty minutes. Broil more tomatoes for the
garnish as the soup is cooking, and serve with Sesame Flat Bread (page 238) and Summer Garden
Salad with Tarragon Vinaigrette (page 177) for a quick and easy summer meal.

1 tablespoon olive oil

1 large yellow onion, coarsely chopped

2 garlic cloves, sliced

4 cups chopped plum tomatoes
   (6–8 large)

4 cups chopped yellow tomatoes
   (4–6 medium)

½ cup chopped celery stalks and leaves

2 tablespoons chopped fresh parsley

1 tablespoon chopped fresh basil

1 teaspoon kosher salt

Broiled Tomatoes (opposite)

Heat the oil in a 4½-quart soup pot. Add the onion and garlic, stirring to coat with the oil. Cover and cook for 3 to 4 minutes, or until the onion begins to soften. Stir in the tomatoes, celery, herbs, and salt. Cover and cook over medium heat for 15 to 20 minutes, or until the celery is tender.

Cool slightly, then use a Foley food mill to puree the soup. Or puree in a food processor or blender and strain through a sieve to remove the seeds and skins. Return to the heat and simmer, uncovered, for 15 minutes, stirring occasionally. Garnish each serving with 3 to 4 slices of the broiled tomatoes.

Serves 4

Ladle, Leaf, & Loaf

~ Broiled Tomatoes ~

These add a little drama and a lot of flavor to soups and can also be served with bread. Olive Bread (page 214) with Green Peppercorn Yogurt Cheese (page 257) topped with Broiled Tomatoes makes a delightful open-faced sandwich.

3 large plum tomatoes

½ teaspoon olive oil

¼ cup freshly grated Parmesan cheese

¼ teaspoon freshly ground black pepper

¼ teaspoon kosher salt

Preheat the oven to 400 degrees. Cut the ends off the tomatoes, and cut each tomato into 4 slices. Arrange them on a small baking sheet. Brush each one with the oil, and sprinkle with the Parmesan, pepper, and salt. Cook for 10 to 12 minutes, or until the cheese melts and the juices bubble. Serve immediately.

Makes enough to garnish 4–6 servings of soup

S AN ARTIST, I trust my visual sensibilities; they're my personal radar system. When I cook, I work my way through my senses, starting with a vision of the dish-to-be. Picturing how the food should look helps me imagine how it should taste, and inspired by these impressions, I'm ready to start creating new dishes. The crisp and delicate Julienned Potatoes are as attractive as they are delicious, proof that it's worthwhile trying to pin down a good idea.

From a strictly culinary point of view, the success of this recipe has a lot to do with food chemistry. Soaking the potatoes draws out their starch. Then, after they're diligently dried, the starchless potatoes absorb the oil and crisp up nicely in the oven. I may have reinvented the wheel when I created this recipe, but my modest little triumph in potatoland proves that art and science can coexist quite nicely in the kitchen.

Roasted Red Pepper Soup
with Crisp Julienned Potatoes

It takes some preparation to make this soup, but the results are
well worth the effort of roasting and peeling the peppers. The soup's
gorgeous color is matched by its unusual flavor.

1½ tablespoons olive oil

2 large red bell peppers, roasted (page 156) and chopped (about 4 cups)

½ cup coarsely chopped yellow onion

3 garlic cloves, sliced

3 cups Chicken Stock (page 32) or canned broth

½ teaspoon crushed pink peppercorns

¼–½ teaspoon kosher salt, to taste

⅛ teaspoon dried rubbed sage
Pinch of ground cloves

Crisp Julienned Potatoes (page 54)

Heat the oil over medium heat in a 4½-quart soup pot. Add the peppers, onion, and garlic, stirring to coat with the oil. Cover and cook for 3 to 4 minutes, or until the vegetables soften. Add the chicken stock. Bring to a boil and reduce the heat to low. Cover and continue cooking for 35 to 40 minutes, or until the peppers are very tender.

Stir in the peppercorns, salt, sage, and cloves. Cook, uncovered, for an additional 10 minutes. Strain, reserving the liquid. Return the liquid to the pot. Puree the vegetables in a food processor. Force the puree through a sieve, and blend with the liquid. Reheat the soup. Garnish each serving with a generous sprinkling of the crisp potatoes.

Serves 4

When I was in college, I loved reading comic books. They weren't exactly edifying, but my favorite line from "Mr. Natural," R. Crumb's goofy, bearded guru, has proved worth remembering: "Use the right tool for the right job!" As far as this recipe goes, a food processor works, but a julienne grater is definitely the right tool for this job.

1 large russet potato, peeled
1 tablespoon olive oil
¼ teaspoon kosher salt

Preheat the oven to 450 degrees. Grate the potato, using a julienne grater or the julienne blade of the food processor, or slice it into very thin matchsticks with a sharp knife. Put the potato in a small bowl, and cover with water. Add a pinch of the salt. Set aside for 5 minutes.

Drain the potatoes thoroughly. Line a large plate with paper towels. Transfer the potatoes to the plate and carefully pat dry. The drier the potatoes, the better the end result. In a small bowl, toss the potatoes with the oil and the rest of the salt.

Spread the potatoes on a large baking sheet and bake for 5 minutes. Use a spatula to stir the potatoes and turn them over. Bake for an additional 5 minutes, stir, and turn again. Crisp for 2 to 3 more minutes. Remove from the oven and use immediately or cool and store in an airtight container. The potatoes will keep refrigerated for 1 to 2 days. Reheat at 450 degrees for about 5 minutes to crisp before serving.

Makes about 1½ cups

Curried Tomato Soup
with Toasted Pumpkin Seeds

IT TAKES LESS THAN AN HOUR to go from the pleasure of inhaling the aroma
of spices cooking in oil to serving this savory tomato soup.

1½ tablespoons olive oil

½ tablespoon curry powder

½ teaspoon ground cumin

Generous pinch of ground cinnamon

Freshly ground black pepper

1 medium yellow onion, quartered
and sliced

1 large garlic clove, sliced

¼ cup water

6 cups coarsely chopped plum tomatoes
(9–12 large)

1 cup Chicken Stock (page 32)
or canned broth

½ teaspoon kosher salt, or to taste

Toasted pumpkin seeds (page 38)

Heat the oil over medium heat in a 4½-quart
soup pot. Add the curry powder, cumin, cinnamon, and pepper, and stir to blend. Add the onion
and garlic, stirring to coat with the spices. Cover
and cook over low heat for 3 to 4 minutes, or until
softened. Add the water and stir in the tomatoes.
Cover and cook for about 30 minutes.

Remove from the heat. Strain, reserving the
vegetables, and return the liquid to the pot. Puree
the vegetables in a food processor. Blend the puree
with the liquid. Stir in the chicken stock, and
reheat the soup. Add the salt. Cook, uncovered,
over low heat, stirring occasionally, for 10 minutes.
Garnish each serving with a sprinkling of the toasted pumpkin seeds.

Serves 4

Herbed Butternut Squash Soup
with Chive and Sweet Red Pepper Yogurt Cheese

SMOOTH, SIMPLE, AND SATISFYING, this soup is one of my autumn and winter favorites. It tastes great served with a few slices of cooked sausage— whatever kind you prefer, either vegetarian or meat.

2 tablespoons olive oil

1 small yellow onion, sliced

2 garlic cloves, coarsely chopped

1 2–pound butternut squash, peeled, seeded, and cut into chunks

1 large carrot, chopped

1 medium red-skinned potato, cut into chunks

3 cups Chicken Stock (page 32) or canned broth

½ teaspoon dried oregano
Kosher salt and freshly ground black pepper to taste

Chive and Sweet Red Pepper Yogurt Cheese (opposite)

Heat the oil in a 4½-quart soup pot over medium heat. Add the onion and garlic, stirring to coat with the oil. Add the squash, carrot, and potato. Cover and cook over low heat until the onions are soft, 3 to 4 minutes. Stir in the chicken stock and oregano. Bring to a boil and reduce the heat to low. Cover and continue cooking for 20 minutes, or until the vegetables can be pierced with a fork.

Cool the soup slightly, and puree in a food processor. Return the puree to the pot and reheat. Stir in the salt and pepper and adjust the seasonings. Garnish each serving with a dollop of the yogurt cheese.

Serves 4

~ Chive and Sweet Red Pepper Yogurt Cheese ~

This decorative condiment goes well with all kinds of pureed vegetable soups.

1 cup **Plain Yogurt Cheese (page 41)**
2½ tablespoons **minced fresh chives**
2½ tablespoons **minced red bell pepper**
Pinch of kosher salt

Mix all the ingredients in a small bowl. To enhance the flavors, refrigerate for at least 1 hour.

Makes about 1¼ cups

Carrot Ginger Soup

THIS PIQUANT GOLDEN-ORANGE SOUP is a vegetarian delight packed with good stuff—vegetables rich in vitamin A. It also boasts a low salt and fat content.

1	tablespoon canola oil
1	large yellow onion, quartered and thinly sliced
2½	cups grated carrots (about 2 large)
1	sweet potato, peeled and cubed
½	tablespoon freshly grated ginger
4½	cups Vegetable Consommé (page 35) or canned vegetable broth
½	teaspoon ground coriander
	Kosher salt to taste

Tamari Almonds (opposite)

Heat the oil over medium heat in a 4½-quart soup pot. Add the onion, stirring to coat with the oil. Cover and cook until the onion starts to soften, 3 to 4 minutes. Stir in the carrots, sweet potato, and ginger and continue cooking for 3 to 4 minutes, or until softened. Add the consommé or canned broth. Stir in the coriander and salt. Bring to a boil, and reduce the heat to low. Cover and continue cooking for about 25 minutes. Uncover and continue to simmer for an additional 35 to 40 minutes, or until the vegetables are very tender.

Strain the soup, reserving the vegetables, and return the liquid to the pot. Puree the vegetables in a food processor. Blend the puree with the liquid and reheat the soup. Serve garnished with a sprinkling of the almonds.

Serves 4

~ Tamari Almonds ~

For flavor, texture, and style, these are a superb addition to soups and salads.

1 cup whole unskinned almonds
1 tablespoon tamari

Preheat the oven to 350 degrees. Spread the almonds on a baking sheet. Drizzle them with the tamari, and stir with a spatula until they are wet. Bake for 5 minutes. Remove from the oven and stir with the spatula. Return to the oven for no longer than 3 minutes; avoid overcooking.

Cool the nuts on the baking sheet, stirring to prevent them from sticking. Store in a tightly lidded jar. The almonds keep for 1 month.

Makes 1 cup

W HY BOTHER TO COOK? It's almost avoidable these days; you can bypass the whole business and go directly to opening packages, pushing buttons on the microwave, cruising the universe of fast food, or eating in restaurants. We all do some of the above, in addition to preparing foods from scratch. It's definitely an eclectic approach, governed by convenience. The irony is that convenience can not only show up at the

kitchen door as a packaged salad, it's also to be found in the dazzling abundance of high-quality food in the supermarket. What to do? Grab the packaged salad, press Speed Dial for takeout, or sign up for cooking classes?

I say cook when you can and take advantage of what's available in the supermarket. There are foods from all over the world on the shelves, and ethnic cookbooks have popped up like road maps. It's astonishing, and yet very easy to take for granted. Our culture is perched on top of the global food chain, and the first ingredient in whatever dish we make or eat ought to be appreciation. Being so far removed from the bare necessity of food as fuel is an enviable position, for which we should be grateful. Appreciation covers a lot of territory, from practicing good nutrition right on through to saving the planet, and there's plenty of room in between for the many joys of cooking.

Potato and Green Chili Soup

SMOOTH AND SPICY, this soup is a blend of some of the classic flavors in Mexican cuisine.

---

1 tablespoon canola oil

1 large yellow onion, coarsely chopped

3 garlic cloves, sliced

¼ cup chopped fresh parsley

¾ teaspoon minced fresh cilantro

½ teaspoon ground cumin

2 4–ounce cans whole mild green
chilies, drained

½ teaspoon kosher salt, or to taste
Freshly ground black pepper

4 cups peeled and coarsely chopped
white-skinned potatoes (4–5 medium)

4½ cups Vegetable Consommé (page 35)
or canned vegetable broth

Cumin-Cilantro Yogurt Cheese
(opposite) or half-and-half
Toasted pine nuts (page 38)

Heat the oil over medium heat in a 4½-quart soup pot. Add the onion, garlic, parsley, and cilantro, stirring to coat with the oil. Mix in the cumin and add the chilies, salt, and pepper. Reduce the heat to low and cook until the onion starts to soften, 3 to 4 minutes. Stir in the potatoes, and add the consommé or canned broth. Bring to a boil. Cover, reduce the heat to medium-low, and cook for about 1 hour, or until the vegetables can be pierced with a fork.

Strain, reserving the vegetables, and return the liquid to the pot. Puree the vegetables in a food processor. Stir the puree into the liquid. Reheat the soup and adjust the seasonings. Garnish each serving with a dollop of the yogurt cheese or a drizzle of the half-and-half and a sprinkling of the toasted pine nuts.

Serves 4–6

~ Cumin-Cilantro Yogurt Cheese ~

The pungent warm flavor of cumin and its leafy counterpart, cilantro, make a zesty combination with yogurt cheese.

1 cup **Plain Yogurt Cheese (page 41)**
⅜ teaspoon **ground cumin**
¾ teaspoon **minced fresh cilantro**
  Finely minced dried red chili, to taste
  Pinch of kosher salt
  Freshly ground black pepper

In a small bowl, stir the yogurt cheese and cumin together. Mix in the remaining ingredients. To enhance the flavors, refrigerate for at least 1 hour.

Makes about 1 cup

Potato-Kale Soup
with Toasted Walnuts

THIS DELICIOUS, FILLING, AND SIMPLE cold weather soup
is of the stick-to-your-ribs variety.

3¼ cups peeled and cubed red-skinned
potatoes (about 3 medium)

¾ cup coarsely chopped yellow onion

¼ cup chopped fresh parsley

1 teaspoon kosher salt

1 small bay leaf
Freshly ground black pepper

4 cups water

1 cup firmly packed, finely shredded kale

½ cup Chicken Stock (page 32)
or canned broth

½ teaspoon dried rubbed sage

½ teaspoon dried oregano

Chopped toasted walnuts (page 38)

Combine the potatoes, onion, parsley, salt, bay leaf, and pepper in a 4½-quart soup pot. Add the water and bring to a boil. Reduce the heat to medium and continue cooking until the vegetables are tender, about 15 minutes. Meanwhile, in a small saucepan, cook the kale in the chicken stock until it wilts, about 5 minutes. Set aside.

Strain the potato mixture, reserving the vegetables, and return the liquid to the pot. Puree the vegetables in a food processor. Stir the puree into the liquid. Stir in the sage and oregano, and simmer, uncovered, over low heat for several minutes.

Stir the cooked kale and any remaining liquid into the soup. Remove the bay leaf. Serve the soup garnished with the toasted walnuts and freshly ground black pepper.

Serves 4

Rich Onion Soup

THIS SOUP is all about onions, ease, elegance, and not too much salt!

2 tablespoons butter

1 bay leaf

1 4–inch sprig fresh thyme

4 cups thinly sliced yellow onions
   (about 4 large)
   Freshly ground black pepper

5½ cups Vegetable Consommé (page 35)
   or canned vegetable broth

¼ cup dry sherry

4 slices Forty-Clove Garlic Bread
   (page 196) or good French bread
   Grated Gruyère cheese

Melt the butter over low heat in a 4½-quart soup pot. Add the bay leaf and thyme. Cover and cook until the herbs become aromatic. Stir in the onions and cook for about 10 minutes, or until they soften. Add the black pepper and then the consommé or canned broth. Cook over medium heat for 5 minutes. Reduce the heat to low, cover, and simmer for 25 to 30 minutes.

Stir in the sherry and cook, uncovered, for 3 to 4 minutes. Garnish each serving with a toasted slice of the bread and a sprinkling of the grated cheese.

Serves 4

Garlic Soup
with Herb and Cheese Croutons

THE IDEA OF GARLIC SOUP might seem a bit much, but cooking garlic transforms its bite into a warm, rich flavor that is tempered by the other ingredients in this recipe.

---

1 cup whole garlic cloves (4–5 bulbs)

1 tablespoon canola oil

2 medium red-skinned potatoes, peeled and cut into 1-inch chunks

1 large carrot, grated

5 cups Vegetable Consommé (page 35) or canned vegetable broth

1½ tablespoons chopped fresh parsley

¼ teaspoon minced fresh cilantro
   Kosher salt and freshly ground black pepper to taste

Herb and Cheese Croutons (opposite)

Peel and slice the garlic. Heat the oil over medium heat in a 4½-quart soup pot. Add the garlic, stirring to coat with the oil. Cover and cook over low heat until the garlic is soft, 3 to 4 minutes. Add the potatoes, carrot, and consommé or canned broth. Bring to a boil. Stir in the parsley and cilantro. Reduce the heat to medium, cover, and simmer for about 1 hour.

Force the soup through a sieve and reheat. Add the salt and pepper. Serve garnished with the croutons.

Serves 4

~ Herb and Cheese Croutons ~

Homemade croutons taste far better than the store-bought kind and don't suffer from the high fat and salt content of processed food. They are also extremely easy to make!

2 cups ½-inch cubes of French Bread (page 198)
    or a store-bought French loaf
1 tablespoon olive oil
½ tablespoon grated Parmesan cheese
¼ teaspoon dried basil
    Freshly ground black pepper

Preheat the oven to 375 degrees. Toss the bread cubes with the oil, Parmesan, basil, and pepper. Spread on a baking sheet. Bake for 8 to 10 minutes, turning frequently with a spatula. Remove from the baking sheet and cool on a plate. The croutons can be stored in a tightly lidded container for several weeks.

Makes 2 cups

Broccoli Cauliflower Soup

THESE CLOSELY RELATED MEMBERS of the cabbage family have their own distinctive tastes, and the aromatic caraway seeds complement them nicely.

- 1 large bunch broccoli
- 1 large head cauliflower
- 1 tablespoon canola oil
- 1 large yellow onion, coarsely chopped
- 1 large garlic clove, thinly sliced
- ½ tablespoon caraway seeds
- 4 cups Chicken Stock (page 32) or canned broth
- ½ teaspoon kosher salt, or to taste

    Cumin and Black Pepper Yogurt Cheese (opposite) or grated Gruyère cheese

Wash and trim the broccoli and cauliflower. Break the florets into small pieces and cut the stems into ½-inch slices. Set aside ½ cup each of the broccoli and cauliflower florets. Cover and refrigerate. Heat the oil over medium heat in a 4½-quart soup pot. Stir in the onion, garlic, and caraway seeds, coating them with the oil. Cover and cook until the onion starts to soften, 3 to 4 minutes.

Add the remaining broccoli and cauliflower to the onion mixture. Stir in the stock and salt. Bring to a boil and reduce the heat to medium-low. Cover and continue cooking for 5 minutes, or until the vegetables can be pierced with a fork.

Strain the vegetables, reserving the broth. Return the broth to the pot. Puree the vegetables in a food processor. Stir the puree into the broth and reheat. Just before serving, add the fresh broccoli and cauliflower florets and reheat again briefly. Serve with a dollop of the yogurt cheese or a sprinkling of the grated Gruyère cheese.

Serves 6

~ Cumin and Black Pepper Yogurt Cheese ~

Yogurt cheese, mixed with warm spices, makes a fine condiment for mild-flavored soups.

1 cup Plain Yogurt Cheese (page 41)
⅜ teaspoon ground cumin
½ tablespoon minced fresh chives
Pinch of turmeric
Pinch of kosher salt
Freshly ground black pepper

In a small bowl, mix the yogurt cheese and cumin. Add the remaining ingredients and mix well. To enhance the flavors, refrigerate for at least 1 hour before serving.

Makes about 1 cup

Pureed Fennel Soup
with Julienned Carrots and Toasted Walnuts

FENNEL IS A CURIOUS VEGETABLE. It looks like the first cousin of both celery and dill, has the bulbous shape of an onion, and tastes like licorice. Regardless of its eccentricities, fennel makes a delicious, subtle soup.

---

1 cup chopped celery

½ cup uncooked white rice

4 cups Chicken Stock (page 32)
    or canned broth

2 fennel bulbs, trimmed and
    coarsely chopped

¼ teaspoon kosher salt

Steamed Julienned Carrots (opposite)
Chopped fresh chives
Toasted walnuts (page 38)

Put the celery, rice, and 1 cup of the chicken stock in a small pot and bring to a boil. Cover, reduce the heat to low, and simmer until the rice is tender, about 10 minutes. Set aside.

Meanwhile, combine the fennel and the remaining 3 cups chicken stock in a 4½-quart soup pot. Add the salt. Bring to a boil and reduce the heat to medium. Cover and continue cooking for 5 minutes, or until the fennel is tender. Strain, reserving the fennel mixture, and return the liquid to the pot. Puree the fennel and the rice mixtures together in a food processor. Force the puree through a sieve, and stir it into the liquid. Reheat the soup. Garnish each serving with a sprinkling of the steamed carrots, chives, and toasted walnuts.

Serves 4–6

Here's a quick and easy way to add a dash of color and texture and a hint of carrot flavor to soups. You can also marinate the carrots in Walnut Oil and Lemon Dressing (page 117) or White Balsamic Vinaigrette (page 121) and use them in salads.

1 **medium carrot, peeled**
1 **bay leaf**

Grate the carrot, using a julienne grater or the julienne blade of the food processor. Place about 2 inches of water in a saucepan large enough to hold a vegetable steamer and put the bay leaf in the water. Place the steamer in the saucepan, add the carrots, cover and steam until tender, about 5 minutes. Remove and use immediately as a garnish for soup or cool and refrigerate. The carrots will keep for several days.

Makes about ¾ cup

❦ CONDIMENTS ❦

ANY COOKS HAVE theatrical aspirations, and like anxious directors and costume designers, we fuss over how we present our creations, adjusting the seasonings and adding the finishing touches just before the food leaves the kitchen. Every dish deserves a little fanfare, and one reason I like condiments so much is that they say "*Voilà!*" for me.

I expect more from condiments than just a decorative flourish, though. Pity poor parsley, forever cast in its lowly role as a garnish, where looks often count more than taste. Every condiment should behave like a garnish and add to the aesthetics of a dish, but it should also resonate with the flavors of the food and enhance them. The texture and temperature of some condiments can be particularly interesting with soups. In cooking, it is often the details that count, and attention to detail is what condiments are all about.

Autumn Vegetable Minestra

THE ITALIAN WORD for "a thick soup" is *minestra*, and this vegetable soup fits the description. Plenty of seasonal ingredients provide substance, while the cannellini beans and plum tomatoes lend a little bit of Italian soul.

2   tablespoons olive oil

1   cup coarsely chopped yellow onion

1   elephant garlic or 2 regular garlic cloves, coarsely chopped

1   cup diagonally sliced carrots

1   cup peeled, seeded, and coarsely chopped delicata or butternut squash

½   cup peeled and sliced parsnips

½   cup red-skinned potato, coarsely chopped

3   cups Vegetable Consommé (page 35) or canned vegetable broth

2   cups sliced portobello mushroom caps

¼   cup dried cannellini beans
    Freshly ground black pepper

2   cups coarsely chopped plum tomatoes (4–6 large)

1   tablespoon chopped fresh parsley

½   teaspoon fresh thyme leaves or ¼ teaspoon dried

1   4-inch sprig fresh marjoram or ½ teaspoon dried

Herb and Cheese Croutons (page 67)

Heat the oil in a 4½-quart soup pot. Add the onion and garlic, stirring to coat with the oil. Cover and cook over low heat until the onion starts to soften, 3 to 4 minutes. Stir in the carrots, squash, parsnips, and potato and cook, covered, for several minutes. Add the consommé or canned broth, mushrooms, beans, and black pepper and increase the heat to medium. Puree the tomatoes in a food processor or blender. Force the puree through a sieve and stir it into the soup. Add the parsley, thyme, and marjoram. Cover and continue cooking for about 1 hour, or until the beans are tender. Serve garnished with the croutons.

Serves 4–6

❧ PUMPKINS ❧

*I*N LATE OCTOBER, the fields near my house with-
draw into the dull tans, grays, and browns that
mark the end of the growing season as the frost
passes through the valley. The deer haunt the hedgerows, and the
herons leave the pond. It would be a bleak time of year if it weren't
for the blazing orange pumpkins sitting smartly on the bare ground,
unfazed by their withered foliage and dried vines.

If a pumpkin finds its way past the porch and into the kitchen, the
cook must decide whether to steam or bake the beast. Both methods
work equally well, tenderizing the pumpkin in preparation for making soups or quick breads. Long Island Cheese Pumpkins have the
correct horticultural pedigree for a puree; they are cultivated for
cooking, although a little kitchen magic is always appreciated.

Ladle, Leaf, & Loaf

Curried Pumpkin Soup

COLD WEATHER, short days, and gray skies—just the right conditions
for serving this well-seasoned, brightly colored soup.

---

1 tablespoon butter

1 cup coarsely chopped yellow onion

1 large garlic clove, sliced

2 teaspoons curry powder

⅛ teaspoon ground cumin

3 cups Chicken Stock (page 32)
   or canned broth

2 cups canned pumpkin or cooked
   and pureed fresh pumpkin

4 teaspoons maple syrup

¼ teaspoon kosher salt

Orange-Zested Yogurt Cheese
   (page 76) or orange slices
Toasted pumpkin seeds (page 38)

Melt the butter in a 4½-quart soup pot. Add the onion and garlic, stirring to coat with the butter, and sprinkle with the curry powder and cumin. Cover and cook over low heat for 3 to 4 minutes, or until the onion starts to soften. Add the chicken stock and stir in the remaining ingredients. Bring to a boil and reduce the heat to low. Continue cooking, uncovered, for 25 to 30 minutes, or until the vegetables are very tender.

Cool slightly. Puree in a food processor. Return the soup to the pot and reheat. Serve garnished with a dollop of the yogurt cheese or thin slices of orange and a sprinkling of the pumpkin seeds.

Serves 4

~ Orange-Zested Yogurt Cheese ~

This condiment adds a bit of citrus and sweetness to the familiar partnership of yogurt and curry.

½ cup Plain Yogurt Cheese (page 41)
    Grated rind of 1 orange
1 teaspoon maple syrup

Mix all the ingredients in a small bowl. To enhance the flavors, refrigerate for at least 1 hour before serving.

Makes about ½ cup

Winter Vegetable Soup

THOSE "KEEPERS" in the vegetable family—the onions and other root vegetables and squashes that store well—make good cold weather soup. Serve with Potato-Onion Rye Bread (page 202) for a satisfying winter meal.

½ tablespoon olive oil

2 medium leeks, with some of
    the green parts, sliced

2 garlic cloves, minced

1 cup chopped savoy cabbage

1 large white-skinned potato,
    cut into small pieces

1 small carrot, sliced

4½ cups Beef Stock (page 33)
    or canned broth

1 medium parsnip, peeled and sliced

1 cup chopped kale

½ cup peeled, seeded, and chopped
    butternut squash

2 tablespoons chopped fresh parsley

1 bay leaf

¼ teaspoon dried thyme leaves

2 tablespoons cider vinegar

¼ teaspoon kosher salt
    Freshly ground black pepper

½ cup minced cooked beef from the soup
    bone used to make Beef Stock (optional)

Freshly grated Parmesan cheese

Heat the oil in a 4½-quart soup pot. Add the leeks and garlic, stirring to coat with the oil. Cover and cook until the vegetables start to soften, about 5 minutes. Add the cabbage, potato, and carrot. Stir in the beef stock. Add the remaining vegetables, herbs, vinegar, salt, and pepper. Bring to a boil, and reduce the heat to medium. Cover and continue cooking for 25 to 30 minutes, or until the vegetables can be pierced with a fork. Remove the lid, stir in the minced beef, and cook, uncovered, for an additional 5 to 10 minutes. Remove the bay leaf, and serve, garnished with a sprinkling of the freshly grated Parmesan.

Serves 4–6

Portobello Mushroom and Barley Soup with Garlic Croutons

MANY YEARS AGO, when I was camping in the English countryside, I used to buy field mushrooms the size of salad plates at the local market. They were filling and inexpensive, having exceeded the limits of what was then considered an acceptable size for a mushroom. Until portobello mushrooms came on the scene, there weren't any others to compare with what I had feasted on in England, and just like those English mushrooms I loved so much, their flavor does not diminish with size.

1½ tablespoons olive oil
1   small yellow onion, minced
1   large garlic clove, pressed
¾   teaspoon kosher salt
    Freshly ground black pepper
¼   cup pearl barley
5½ cups cubed portobello mushroom caps
    (about 1 pound)
¼   cup chopped fresh parsley
½   tablespoon fresh thyme leaves
    or ¼ teaspoon dried
4   cups water
3   tablespoons medium-dry sherry

Garlic Croutons (opposite)

Heat the oil over medium heat in a 4½-quart soup pot. Add the onion, garlic, salt, and pepper. Stir in the barley, coating it with the oil. Reduce the heat to low and cook for 5 minutes, stirring frequently. Add the mushrooms, parsley, thyme, and water. Bring to a boil and reduce the heat to medium. Cover and continue cooking for about 1½ hours, or until the barley is soft. Stir in the sherry and cook, uncovered, for an additional 10 minutes. Garnish with the croutons and serve.

Serves 4

~ Garlic Croutons ~

If you use Forty-Clove Garlic Bread, there's no need to add extra garlic: it's in the bread, and it makes these croutons extremely simple to prepare.

- 3 garlic cloves, pressed
- 1 tablespoon olive oil
- 2 cups cubed French Bread (page 198), Forty-Clove Garlic Bread (page 196), or a store-bought French loaf
- ¼ teaspoon kosher salt
  Freshly ground black pepper

Preheat the oven to 375 degrees. Sauté the garlic in the oil in a small skillet over medium heat until soft, about 2 minutes.

In a medium bowl, toss the bread cubes with the garlic mixture, salt, and pepper. Spread the croutons on a baking sheet. Bake for 8 to 10 minutes, turning frequently with a spatula. Remove from the baking sheet and cool on a plate. The croutons can be stored in a tightly lidded container for several weeks.

Makes 2 cups

Ladle, Leaf, & Loaf

Soups with Lentils, Beans, and Peas

EVERYBODY KNOWS THAT LEGUMES are the good guys in the vegetable kingdom because they are a source of protein. It is no wonder, then, that the lowly bean is given magic powers in fairy tales; even without USDA food pyramids, it was clear long ago that a handful of beans is worth more than meets the eye. Magic and nutritional value aside, I like them for their stick-to-your-ribs heartiness. These recipes include the speediest stove-to-table dry legume there is, the red lentil (also known as "dal"), and, in increasing order of cooking time, lentils, assorted dry beans, and peas.

Ladle, Leaf, & Loaf

Curried Lentil Soup

LENTILS ORIGINATED in central Asia, where some clever cook discovered the appetizing results of seasoning them with curry powder. That was a long time ago, but it still works.

---

1 cup green lentils, sorted and rinsed

4 cups Vegetable Consommé (page 35) or canned vegetable broth

3 small carrots, sliced on the diagonal

1 cup cubed new potatoes

½ cup thinly sliced Vidalia onion

2 garlic cloves, sliced

2 tablespoons chopped fresh parsley

1 tablespoon chopped fresh chives

½ teaspoon curry powder

½ teaspoon caraway seeds

Freshly ground black pepper and kosher salt to taste

Minted Yogurt Cheese

Combine the lentils and consommé or canned broth in a 4½-quart soup pot and bring to a boil. Reduce the heat to low, and stir in the remaining ingredients. Cover and simmer for about 45 minutes, or until the lentils are soft. Adjust the seasonings, and serve with a dollop of the yogurt cheese.

Serves 4–6

~ Minted Yogurt Cheese ~

Cool and refreshing, Minted Yogurt Cheese is a good match for the spices in Curried Lentil Soup.

1 cup Plain Yogurt Cheese (page 41)

1¼ teaspoons minced fresh mint

1 teaspoon honey

In a small bowl, stir the yogurt cheese and mint together. Add the honey and mix well. To enhance the flavors, refrigerate for at least 1 hour before serving.

Makes about 1 cup

Lentil Soup with Hijiki and Braised Tofu

THIS LENTIL SOUP makes a delicious turn toward the East—flavored with miso, ginger, just a taste of smoky hijiki seaweed, and a hint of five-spice powder in the tofu garnish.

1½ tablespoons dried hijiki seaweed

½ tablespoon canola oil

½ tablespoon sesame oil

1 medium yellow onion, thinly sliced

⅔ cup finely chopped carrots

1 large garlic clove, thinly sliced

½ teaspoon freshly grated ginger

2 tablespoons miso paste

4 cups water, plus ½ cup hot water

⅔ cup green lentils, sorted and rinsed

Braised Tofu (opposite)

In a small bowl, cover the hijiki with boiling water. Let it sit for 20 minutes. Drain, rinse, and cover with more hot water. Set aside.

Heat the oils over medium heat in a 4½-quart soup pot. Add the onion, carrots, garlic, and ginger, stirring to coat with the oil. Cover and cook over low heat for 3 to 4 minutes, until the vegetables start to soften.

In a small bowl, dissolve the miso paste in the ½ cup hot water, and stir it into the soup. Add the lentils and the remaining 4 cups water. Bring to a boil and reduce the heat to medium. Cover and continue cooking for 30 minutes. Drain the hijiki and add it to the soup. Cover and cook the soup for an additional 15 minutes, or until the lentils are tender. Garnish each serving with a slice of the braised tofu.

Serves 4

~ Braised Tofu ~

Here is a simple dish that brings out the best in this excellent but low-key source of protein.

- 1 teaspoon peanut oil
- ½ teaspoon sesame oil
- 1 large garlic clove, pressed
- ¼ teaspoon five-spice powder (available in Asian markets)
- 4–6 slices firm tofu, 2 x 3 x ¼ inches each
- 1 teaspoon tamari

In a medium skillet, stir together the oils, garlic, and five-spice powder and cook over medium heat for about 3 minutes until aromatic. Add the tofu, turning to coat with the oil mixture. Cover and cook for 5 minutes. Add the tamari and cook, uncovered, for an additional 5 minutes, turning the tofu occasionally. Use immediately as a garnish for the hot soup.

Makes enough to garnish 4–6 servings of soup

Red Lentil and Kale Soup

WITH THE PROTEIN-PACKED LENTILS and vitamin-rich kale on board, this is a very nutritious soup; the mustard adds a pleasant undercurrent of warmth and spice to the broth.

---

1 tablespoon olive oil

1 small yellow onion, minced

4 garlic cloves, pressed

4½ cups Vegetable Consommé (page 35)
or canned vegetable broth

2 cups finely chopped kale

½ cup thinly sliced carrots

½ cup red lentils, sorted and rinsed
Freshly ground black pepper and
kosher salt to taste

3 teaspoons prepared mustard

Chopped toasted walnuts (page 38)

Heat the oil over medium heat in a 4½-quart soup pot. Add the onion and garlic, stirring to coat with the oil. Cover and cook until the onion starts to soften, 3 to 4 minutes. Add ½ cup of the vegetable consommé or broth. Stir in the kale and carrots. Cover and cook until the kale wilts, about 5 minutes.

Add the remaining 4 cups consommé or broth, the lentils, pepper, and salt. In a small dish blend the mustard with some of the liquid from the soup and add the mixture to the soup. Bring to a boil and reduce the heat to low. Cover and continue cooking until the lentils are tender, about 40 minutes. Serve garnished with a sprinkling of the toasted walnuts.

Serves 4

Twelve-Bean Soup
with Herb and Cheese Croutons

THIS SOUP PROVES that a handful of beans and an assortment of herbs can make
good soup without a beef bone or ham hock, thank you very much—
going vegetarian all the way works just fine!

1 tablespoon olive oil

1 large yellow onion, coarsely chopped

1 elephant garlic clove or 2 regular
   cloves, minced

3 sprigs fresh thyme

2 fresh sage leaves
   1½-inch sprig fresh rosemary

1 tablespoon chopped fresh parsley

1 cup mixed dried beans (equal parts
   yellow and green split peas, garbanzo,
   black, navy, and kidney beans, or use
   a packaged assortment), sorted
   and rinsed

6 cups water

¾ teaspoon kosher salt
   Freshly ground black pepper

Herb and Cheese Croutons (page 67)

Heat the oil over medium heat in a 4½-quart
soup pot. Add the onion and garlic, stirring to coat
with the oil. Cover and cook until the vegetables
soften, 3 to 4 minutes. Stir in the herbs. Cover and
cook for 3 to 4 minutes, until they become aromatic. Add the beans, water, salt, and pepper.
Bring to a boil, reduce the heat to medium-low,
cover, and cook for about 1 hour, or until the
beans are tender. Serve garnished with the croutons.

Serves 4–6

Carrot and Cannellini Bean Soup with Cumin

MY AUSTRALIAN SISTER-IN-LAW taught me how to make this soup,
and it has become a family tradition.

---

1 cup dried cannellini beans, sorted
  and rinsed
1 tablespoon olive oil
1 large yellow onion, coarsely chopped
1 garlic clove, minced
2½ cups grated carrots (about 2 large)
6 cups Vegetable Consommé (page 35)
  or canned vegetable broth
1 large bay leaf
1 teaspoon kosher salt
  Freshly ground black pepper

  Cumin and Black Pepper Yogurt
  Cheese (page 69) or grated cheddar
  cheese

Cover the beans with water in a medium saucepan. Cover, bring to a boil, and remove from the heat. Set aside to soak for 4 hours.

Heat the oil over medium heat in a 4½-quart soup pot. Add the onion and garlic. Reduce the heat to low, cover, and cook until the vegetables soften, 3 to 4 minutes. Stir in the carrots. Cover and cook for 3 to 4 minutes. Drain the beans and add them to the vegetable mixture. Stir in the consommé or broth and add the bay leaf, salt, and pepper. Bring to a boil, reduce the heat to medium, and cook for 1½ hours, or until the beans are tender. Remove the bay leaf. Serve with a sprinkling of the yogurt cheese or grated cheddar.

Serves 4–6

Split Pea and Tomato Soup with Garlic

I REMEMBER EATING canned split pea and canned tomato soup mixed together when I was a kid, and I loved it. Here is the grown-up version of my childhood favorite.

⅔ cup dried split peas, sorted and rinsed

7 cups water

4 cups coarsely chopped plum tomatoes (8–10 large)

1 large carrot, sliced

1 small yellow onion, chopped

1 large garlic clove, minced

¼ cup chopped fresh parsley

½ tablespoon fresh thyme leaves

1 bay leaf

1 teaspoon kosher salt

Freshly ground black pepper

1 large garlic clove, pressed

½ cup chopped sun-dried tomatoes

In a small bowl, cover the split peas with 2 cups of the water. Set aside to soak for 2 hours.

In a 4½-quart soup pot, mix together the tomatoes and 2½ cups of the water. Bring to a boil and reduce the heat to medium. Cover and continue cooking until the tomatoes start to soften, about 5 minutes. Drain the peas and add to the soup pot with the remaining 2½ cups water. Stir in all the remaining ingredients except the pressed garlic and sun-dried tomatoes.

Bring to a boil, reduce the heat to low, cover, and cook for about 2 hours, or until the peas are tender. Cool slightly and puree the soup in a food processor. Return to the pot, and cook over low heat for about 30 minutes. Meanwhile, soak the sun-dried tomatoes in boiling water to cover until they are soft, about 10 minutes; drain. Just before serving, stir the pressed garlic and the tomatoes into the soup.

Serves 4–6

Chilled Soups

CHILLED SOUP can't be wimpy. Low-key and low temperature add up to low-grade in my opinion; without distinctive qualities, chilled soups just aren't very interesting. These recipes include generous amounts of seasonings that don't lose their character when the temperature goes down. The textures of a smooth puree or a refreshing light broth are very appealing when they are cold, especially with the addition of lightly steamed vegetables or crisp fresh ones—and the sparkling colors and elegant appearance of these soups are an invitation to dine.

Gazpacho with Fresh Tarragon

THIS GAZPACHO has visible vegetables and crisp layers of flavor; it is not one of the homogenized varieties that are made in a blender and taste like confused salsa.

3 pounds tomatoes, coarsely chopped, plus 2 medium tomatoes, seeded and cut into bite-sized pieces

1 cucumber, peeled and seeded

2 garlic cloves

1 tablespoon white balsamic vinegar

¾ teaspoon kosher salt
Freshly ground black pepper

1 tablespoon olive oil

½ green bell pepper, cut into bite-sized pieces

½ yellow pepper, cut into bite-sized pieces

½ cup minced red onion

Fresh tarragon leaves

Puree the 3 pounds tomatoes, half of the cucumber, and the garlic in a food processor. Strain over a large bowl; discard the skins and seeds. Stir the vinegar, salt, and pepper into the juice.

Finely chop the remaining half of the cucumber. Add the cucumber, the 2 cut-up tomatoes, and the peppers and onion to the bowl. Chill thoroughly. Garnish each serving with several of the fresh tarragon leaves.

Serves 4

Chilled Zucchini and Carrot Soup

THIS IS MY FAVORITE KIND OF RECIPE. It proves you don't need much in the way of ingredients or time to make good food; it's how you put it all together that counts.

---

1 tablespoon olive oil

1 medium yellow onion, thinly sliced

1 large garlic clove, thinly sliced

1 tablespoon minced fresh chives

1 tablespoon chopped fresh parsley

1 tablespoon chopped fresh basil

½ teaspoon fresh thyme leaves

Freshly ground black pepper

4 cups sliced small tender zucchini
   (2–3 whole)

2 cups water

1 teaspoon kosher salt

2 cups diagonally sliced carrots

Sliced scallions

Heat the oil over medium heat in a 4½-quart soup pot. Add the onion and garlic, stirring to coat with the oil. Add the herbs and black pepper. Cover and cook until the onion starts to soften, 3 to 4 minutes. Add the zucchini, water, and salt. Bring to a boil and reduce the heat to medium. Cover and continue cooking until the vegetables are tender, about 5 minutes. Set aside to cool for 10 minutes. Meanwhile, steam the carrots until tender and set aside.

Strain the zucchini mixture over a medium bowl, reserving the vegetables, and return the liquid to the pot. Puree the zucchini in a food processor, and stir the puree into the liquid.

Add the steamed carrots to the soup and chill thoroughly. Garnish each serving with the sliced scallions.

Serves 6

Chilled Fresh Green Pea Soup

I AM CONVINCED that this soup is what the color green tastes like.

---

1   tablespoon olive oil
1   cup thinly sliced Vidalia onion
1   garlic clove, sliced
2   cups shelled fresh green peas
½   tablespoon minced fresh mint
⅛   teaspoon crushed green peppercorns
3½ cups Chicken Stock (page 32)
    or canned broth
    Kosher salt to taste

Minted Yogurt Cheese (page 81)
Chopped fresh chives

Heat the oil over medium heat in a 4½-quart soup pot. Add the onion and garlic, stirring to coat with the oil. Cover and cook until they soften, 3 to 4 minutes. Stir in the peas and mint, and add 1 cup of the stock and the peppercorns. Cover and cook for 5 minutes.

Transfer the mixture to a food processor and puree thoroughly. Force the puree through a sieve into a medium bowl, adding ½ cup of the stock to the mixture in the sieve when it starts to become dry. Blend in the remaining 2 cups stock into the puree and adjust the seasonings. Refrigerate the soup until thoroughly chilled. Serve, garnished with a dollop of the yogurt cheese and a sprinkling of the chives.

Serves 4

Chilled White Potato Soup with Cilantro and Cumin-Chili Croutons

A SOUTH-OF-THE-BORDER interpretation of the classic vichyssoise.

1 tablespoon canola oil

1 bunch scallions, white parts only, thinly sliced

1 large white onion, thinly sliced

4 cups peeled and cubed white-skinned potatoes (4–5 medium)

¼ cup chopped fresh flat-leaf parsley

¼ cup chopped fresh cilantro

4 cups Vegetable Consommé (page 35) or canned vegetable broth

Cumin-Chili Croutons (opposite)

Heat the oil over medium heat in a 4½-quart soup pot. Add the scallions and onion, stirring to coat with the oil. Cover and cook until the vegetables start to soften, 3 to 4 minutes. Stir in the potatoes and herbs and add the consommé or broth. Bring the soup to a boil. Reduce the heat to low, cover, and cook until the vegetables are tender, about 20 minutes.

Strain the vegetables over a large bowl, reserving the vegetables, and return the liquid to the pot. Puree the vegetables in a food processor. Force the puree through a sieve and blend with the liquid. Refrigerate the soup until thoroughly chilled. Garnish each serving with some of the croutons.

Serves 6

Ladle, Leaf, & Loaf

~ Cumin-Chili Croutons ~

These spicy croutons perk up soups and salads; try them with Split Pea and Tomato Soup with Garlic (page 87) or Herbed Butternut Squash Soup (page 56).

2 cups ½-inch cubes of French Bread (page 198)
   or a store-bought French loaf
1 tablespoon canola oil
½ teaspoon dried chives
¼ teaspoon ground cumin
¼ teaspoon chili powder
¼ teaspoon kosher salt
   Freshly ground black pepper

Toss the bread cubes with the oil, chives, and spices. Spread on a baking sheet. Bake for 8 to 10 minutes, or until lightly browned, turning frequently with a spatula. Remove from the baking sheet and cool on a plate. The croutons can be stored in a tightly lidded container for several weeks.

Makes 2 cups

I'VE NOTICED A PHENOMENON in my daily life that I call the ebb and flow of domestic tranquility. What it describes is the perpetual shift between order and chaos in the household: from clean countertops and not a dish in sight to having to forage for a spoon in the dishwasher and wash it because the silverware drawer is empty. Or the laundry! How often are the hampers empty, the washing machine and dryer silent, and the clothes folded and put away all at the same time?

My studio can't buck the trend, either. When I get going on a project, the level of chaos rises in direct proportion to my level of immersion. The deeper I go, the less attention I pay to the wake I leave behind. It's so messy, though! Scraps of paper all over the table and floor, other pieces with glue on them that stick to my socks, scissors set aside for just a moment and then buried beneath the clutter, piles of reference books all over the place—a wanton display of creative abandon.

Whether I'm reaching for my apron or rummaging around in the studio looking in the flat file for paper, the maintenance agreement remains the same: Get everything back to square one when the project's over so each new effort starts on an equal footing. Cyclical good housekeeping, in other words. A great deal of preparing food, doing housework, and making art falls into the realm of the mundane. Inspiration may arrive like a bolt out of the blue, but it's not going to be of much use without the work that's required to transform an artistic vision into a concrete object. Labor is greatly undervalued when it comes to housework and romanticized when it comes to art. Harnessing creativity is a big job, and the mystery of it is that something as mundane as labor can be an integral part of such a transcendent experience.

A delicious meal from a kitchen that is left in a shambles and the piece of artwork that emerges fully formed from a messy studio are the rewards of pursuing a vision and capturing it. The fact that there's a mess to clean up afterward is just a reminder of how real the experience has been, and it gives one some time to savor the outcome. At least that's the explanation I've come up with to rationalize my eccentric work habits.

Art has a life of its own, with more longevity than a good meal, perhaps, but they both come from a creative impulse that's governed by the ebb and flow of order and chaos. Keeping up with this process is challenging enough without the added burden of assigning some kind of mental rating system for activities: sorting socks, three points; creating an illustration, four points; making a successful soufflé—off the chart! I like to keep it simple and lump everything together under a heading that says, All in a Day's Work.

Chilled Beet Soup with Beet Greens

I LIKE BORSCHT with a beet flavor and freshness that match the intensity of the beet-colored broth, and the only way to accomplish that is to use very young vegetables. The soup should be served in wide, shallow bowls to show off the beauty of the ingredients.

10–12   **baby beets, about the size of golf balls**

6½   **cups water**

½   **cup firmly packed chopped cleaned beet greens**

1½   **tablespoons dark brown sugar**

5–6   **tablespoons freshly squeezed and strained lemon juice**

½–¾   **teaspoons kosher salt, to taste**

1   **small white onion, finely grated**

3   **large hard-boiled eggs, peeled**

6–12   **new potatoes (golf ball–sized or smaller), boiled**

  Plain Yogurt Cheese (page 41) or sour cream

  Chopped fresh dill

  Chopped fresh chives

Scrub the beets and cover with the water in a 4½-quart soup pot. Bring to a boil and spoon off the scum. Reduce the heat to medium and cook until the beets are tender, 25 to 30 minutes.

Strain the liquid from the cooked beets into a large bowl. Immediately add the beet greens to the hot liquid. Immerse the beets in cold water, slip off the skins, drain, and set aside. Stir the brown sugar, lemon juice, salt, and onion into the beet liquid. Adjust the seasonings. Slice the beets into small pieces and add them to the soup. Cover and refrigerate until completely chilled.

Add half of a hard-boiled egg and 1 or 2 boiled potatoes to each serving. Garnish each serving with a dollop of the yogurt cheese or sour cream and a sprinkling of the dill and chives.

Serves 6

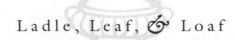

Melting Pot Soups

OUR CULTURE HAS REMARKABLE POWERS of absorption and a rapid turnaround time when an idea takes hold. When news travels fast, things can get lost in the translation or be deliberately altered on the way down the grapevine. If the hot item is a new cuisine, the mutations can get interesting. The story often starts with the words "This is the way my grandmother in Sicily made . . ." (Substitute Mexico, Taiwan, or Uganda for Sicily.) And inevitably, authenticity yields to adaptation, and the cook goes on to say something like, "My mother added tomatoes, and I left out the butter . . ." Regardless of whether or not we are paying homage to Grandma, it's the exposure to new foods or different ways of cooking familiar ingredients that's important.

Quick Miso Soup with Butternut Squash and Scallions

Miso soup is a comfort food with restorative properties that remind me of chicken soup. It can also be part of an elegant meal.

¼ cup crumbled dried wakame seaweed

6 cups water

1 dashi tea bag

4 tablespoons miso paste

⅓ cup ½-inch cubes peeled
    butternut squash

½ cup ½-inch cubes silken tofu

3 tablespoons sliced scallions

Slivers of daikon radish

Put the seaweed in a small bowl, cover with boiling water, and set aside to soak for 15 minutes, or until softened. Drain.

Bring the 6 cups water to a boil in a 4½-quart soup pot. Add the dashi tea bag and reduce the heat to low. Cover and simmer for 10 minutes. Remove the bag, pressing out the excess liquid over the pot. Whisk the miso into the broth. Add the squash. Cover, increase the heat to medium, and cook for about 15 minutes, or until the squash is tender. Add the tofu, scallions, and drained seaweed. Cook for several minutes over medium heat. Serve garnished with the slivers of daikon radish.

Serves 4

Posole with Chicken

POSOLE is a meal in a bowl. Serve with Green Chili Corn Bread (page 218).

5   cups Chicken Stock (page 32) or
    canned broth
1   15–ounce can hominy
1   medium yellow onion, chopped
3   tomatillos, husked and sliced
¼   cup minced red bell pepper
1   tablespoon chopped fresh cilantro
    leaves
1   ¼-inch-square piece dried red chili
¼   teaspoon dried oregano
1   cup diced cooked white-meat chicken
    Freshly ground black pepper and
    kosher salt, to taste

Toasted pine nuts (page 38)

Heat the stock or broth in a 4½-quart soup pot over medium heat. Stir in the hominy, onion, tomatillos, and red pepper. Add the cilantro, chili, and oregano. Cover and cook over low heat for about 1 hour. Add the chicken, and season with the black pepper and salt and heat briefly. Garnish with the pine nuts and serve.

Serves 4–6

Beet and Cabbage Soup

In 1954, it was a long, long drive from New Mexico, where my family lived, to the end of the boardwalk near Coney Island, where my grandmother lived. In spite of feeling as though I'd traveled from one universe to another, I was always comfortable in my grandmother's kitchen; she cooked from the heart and called me "darling" with a Yiddish accent and served us hot borscht. My mother made her own version of it, and this—in keeping with that familial continuity food gives us—is my contribution to the pot.

---

5 cups Beef Stock (page 33)
2 cups peeled and diced beets
1½ cups chopped savoy cabbage
1 cup peeled, cubed white-skinned potato
½ cup sliced carrots
½ cup firmly packed chopped beet greens
1 small yellow onion, sliced
Kosher salt to taste

Dilled Yogurt Cheese or sour cream

Combine the ingredients in a 4½-quart soup pot. Bring to a boil, cover, reduce the heat to low, and simmer for 1 hour, or until the vegetables are soft. Serve with a dollop of the yogurt cheese or sour cream.

Serves 4–6

Dilled Yogurt Cheese

1¼ teaspoons minced fresh dill
1 cup Plain Yogurt Cheese (page 41)
Generous ¼ teaspoon crushed
red peppercorns
Pinch of kosher salt

In a small bowl, stir the dill into the yogurt cheese. Add the peppercorns and salt and mix well. To enhance the flavors, refrigerate for at least 1 hour before serving.

Makes about 1 cup

Pine Nut Porridge with Mint Leaves

I WAS INTRODUCED to pine nut porridge in a Korean restaurant and was determined to try to figure out how to make it myself. Since I'm not familiar with Korean cuisine, once I got the texture and consistency of the soup as I remembered it, I seasoned it with the flavors I always associate with pine nuts from my southwestern background.

1 tablespoon canola oil

1 medium yellow onion, sliced

6 cups Chicken Stock (page 32) or canned broth

¾ cup pine nuts

¾ cup quick-cooking rolled oats

¼ cup chopped fresh parsley

1 large fresh sage leaf

1 tablespoon fresh chopped mint or ½ teaspoon dried mint

1 1¼-inch-square piece dried red chili

Freshly ground black pepper

Kosher salt, to taste

Fresh mint leaves (optional)

Heat the oil over medium heat in a 4½-quart soup pot. Add the onion, stir to coat with the oil, and cook until it starts to soften, 3 to 4 minutes. Add the chicken stock, pine nuts, and oats. Reduce the heat to low, cover, and cook for 30 minutes. Add the parsley, sage, and mint. Cook for an additional 30 minutes. Puree the soup in a food processor and reheat. Add the pepper and salt. Garnish with fresh mint leaves, if desired.

Serves 4–6

Golden Lemon Chicken Soup
with Egg Noodles

HOMEMADE STOCK is essential for this smooth and sassy chicken soup.
You can serve it by candlelight, and it will still cure what ails you.

½ cup uncooked white rice

½ cup chopped celery stalks and leaves

1 small carrot, sliced

5 cups Chicken Stock (page 32)

2 tablespoons freshly squeezed and
strained lemon juice

1 tablespoon minced fresh parsley

¼ teaspoon kosher salt

2 cups cooked Egg Noodles (opposite)

1½ cups diced cooked chicken (optional)

In a small saucepan, combine the rice, celery, carrot, and 1 cup of the stock. Bring the mixture to a boil. Cover and reduce the heat to low. Cook for about 10 minutes, or until the rice has absorbed the liquid. Heat the remaining 4 cups of stock in a 4½-quart soup pot.

Puree the cooked rice in a food processor. Force the mixture through a sieve into the chicken stock. Stir in the lemon juice, parsley, salt, and cooked noodles. Add the chicken (if desired), heat briefly, and serve.

Serves 4

Ladle, Leaf, & Loaf

~ Egg Noodles ~

Roll up your sleeves and relax! Homemade noodles are impressive, but not impossible. The only trick to great noodles is rolling the dough very thin, which a pasta machine can do to a fare-thee-well. If you don't have a pasta machine, a smooth surface, a rolling pin, and pressure can do a very fine job, indeed. Don't despair—just think flat!

2 extra-large eggs
1 teaspoon kosher salt
½ teaspoon dried basil
1¼ cups all-purpose flour

In a small bowl, beat the eggs with the salt and basil. Gradually stir in 1 cup of the flour. Transfer the dough to a lightly floured surface, and knead in the remaining ¼ cup flour. Place the dough in a lightly oiled bowl, cover with plastic wrap, and set aside to rest for 1 hour. Meanwhile, fill a large pot with water and bring to a boil.

Divide the dough into quarters. On a lightly floured surface, roll out each piece of dough until it is very, very thin, or use a pasta machine. Slice the dough with a knife or the pasta machine into ribbons about ⅜ inch wide and 2 inches long. Drop the noodles into the rapidly boiling water. Cook, stirring, until the noodles are just tender, 2 to 3 minutes. Drain and add to your soup.

Uncooked noodles can be stored in the refrigerator for several days or dried for future use. To refrigerate, dust the noodles with flour. Transfer them to sheets of wax paper, and cut the paper to fit inside a zipper-lock bag. Make several layers of noodles. To dry the noodles, transfer them to lightly floured sheets of wax paper and leave them at room temperature for several hours, until stiff. Shake off the flour and store in a tightly lidded jar.

Makes 4 cups cooked noodles

WHENEVER I THINK ABOUT INGREDIENTS, the "Know Your Ingredients" section of *The Joy of Cooking* comes to mind. Many years ago, when I first read through its pages, I was intimidated by the scope of the information. History! Food science! Substitutions and equivalents! This was serious business. Confronted with my own ignorance, I put the book aside. The more I cooked, the less I worried about being fluent in food facts. I moved into a hands-on phase of learning in the kitchen and stopped looking over my shoulder as if the food police were hot on my trail because "vanilla

bean . . . orchid . . . Madagascar" weren't on the tip of my tongue.

Eventually, all that cooking led me back to "Know Your Ingredients." I was ready to learn more about what I was slicing, dicing, mincing, chopping, blending, pulverizing, straining, and experimenting with in my kitchen. When "Know Your Ingredients" fell short, I latched on to the *Larousse Gastronomique,* and I haven't let go since. Trimalchio's feast with thrushes flying forth from the belly of a roasted wild boar! Ninety-five recipes for clear soups! Twelve pages of exhaustive descriptions of offal, politely called "variety meats," and lessons on cleaning flounder. It's a real page-turner and has transformed me into a devotee of food facts. The food police would be proud.

Seafood Soups

F YOU COME OVER FOR DINNER and I serve you any of these seafood soups, it means that I really like you a lot. They take a little more time to prepare, and the ingredients are more expensive than most of the others called for in this book. I have to be in the mood to make these soups. If I'm at the grocery store the day the fish is delivered and inspiration strikes, I hurry home with fresh seafood and start cooking. But don't worry. If you come over knowing this and are served Potato-Kale Soup instead, we can still be friends.

Shrimp Bisque

"Bisques . . . have always been considered high-style preparations."
That declaration from *Larousse Gastronomique* certainly bumps this soup right up there
into first class, but don't assume that Shrimp Bisque is difficult or laden
with calories—it's easy to prepare and low in fat.

---

6 cups water

2 Dashi tea bags

1 medium leek, white part only, sliced

1 10-inch stalk lemongrass,
    cut into thirds

2 tablespoons chopped fresh parsley

1 small garlic clove, pressed

½ pound medium shrimp, peeled
    and deveined

⅓ cup cooked white rice (from about
    3 tablespoons uncooked)

Tamari Almonds (page 59)

In a 4½-quart soup pot, bring the water to a boil. Add the dashi tea bags, cover, and cook for 10 minutes. Remove the tea bags, pressing out the excess liquid over the pot. Remove 1 cup of the broth, place in a small skillet, and set aside.

Add the leek, lemongrass, and parsley to the pot. Cook, covered, for 10 minutes.

Heat the reserved broth until it simmers. Stir in the garlic and add the shrimp. Cook the shrimp, turning them over as they cook, for about 5 minutes, until they are pink. Remove from the heat, drain the liquid into a small cup, and set the shrimp aside.

Remove the lemongrass from the broth and discard. Add the rice and the liquid from the shrimp, and heat, uncovered, for several minutes. Strain, reserving the broth. Puree the vegetables, rice, and 7 or 8 of the reserved shrimp in a food processor until the mixture is very smooth. Force through a sieve and stir into the broth. Cut the remaining shrimp in half lengthwise, add them to the soup, reheat., and serve garnished with almonds.

Serves 4

CURIOSITY IS SOMETHING ARTISTS GET USED TO—that is, other people's curiosity about their work. "How did you do that?" "What does it mean?" And the worst one: "Why do you make things like that?" It's an odd situation, being asked to discuss a nonverbal form of expression. The darned work is supposed to "speak" for itself! You have to develop a party line and be willing to help people out with some sort of explanation. After all, for some folks, looking at artwork can feel a bit like going to a social gathering and trying to make conversation with a stranger. The question "What do you do?" pops up because it's a safe place to start.

The question I am most often asked about my artwork is "How do you do that? With a knife?" The fact that I use scissors instead of knives surprises people, and I use the question as an opportunity to explain that cutting paper is like sculpting, only with a very thin medium. Like sculpture, cutting paper is a process of addition or subtraction to make an image, and it uses positive and negative spaces to define forms. It's easy to see this principle in my work, and I tell people that experimenting with this technique is like playing a game. For instance, if I want to make an apple, I can cut out the silhouette of an apple. Or, I can make the same silhouette and then cut out the center of the image to make an apple that looks like a line drawing. Any sense of color, weight, and texture that I'm trying to suggest all depend on how effectively I can make those snips, holes, outlines, and cut-paper shapes communicate.

What motivates me to work in the studio and the process that takes place there are very private matters, but I'm happy to share the results with the public.

I avoid the "why" questions like the plague. Suppose I pick up a pebble on the beach because I think it's pretty. I show it to you, and you agree. We can talk about the pleasing colors and the shape of the pebble, but there's no need for me to justify its existence with a geology lesson. If I can convince you to look at the pebbles on the beach in an entirely new way, I've done my job as an artist.

Saffron Salmon Chowder with Sweet Peppers

FRESH FISH, FRESH FISH STOCK, FINE SOUP . . . that's what you'll end up with if you boldly venture forth and make the stock from the salmon and use the fillets in this soup.

6 cups Fish Stock (page 34)

2 pounds fresh salmon fillets, cut into bite-sized pieces

2 cups peeled and cubed white-skinned potatoes

2 tablespoons minced shallots

½ teaspoon kosher salt

¼ teaspoon saffron threads

2 heaping tablespoons chopped celery leaves

1 tablespoon chopped fresh parsley

¾ cup dried bread crumbs

Freshly ground black pepper

Slivers of red bell and orange bell peppers

Heat the stock in a 4½-quart soup pot. Add the fish, potatoes, shallots, salt, and saffron. Bring to a boil, reduce the heat to low, cover, and cook for 20 minutes. Add the celery leaves, parsley, and bread crumbs. Cover and cook until the potatoes are tender and the bread crumbs have been absorbed. Add the black pepper and adjust the seasonings. Garnish with the bell peppers and serve.

Serves 4

Ladle, Leaf, & Loaf

Scallop Chowder with Lime Juice

COOKING THE SCALLOPS just briefly in lime juice and olive oil and then adding them to the soup for a mere ten minutes before serving keeps these delicate shellfish tender and succulent.

2 tablespoons olive oil

4 cups bite-sized pieces of peeled red-skinned potatoes (4 medium)

1 medium yellow onion, thinly sliced

¼ cup minced fresh parsley

5¼ cups Vegetable Consommé (page 35) or canned vegetable broth

¼ cup freshly squeezed and strained lime juice

4 fresh basil leaves, chopped

¼ teaspoon crushed green peppercorns

1 pound fresh scallops

¾ cup dried bread crumbs

Slivers of fresh lime

Heat 1 tablespoon of the oil over medium heat in a 4½-quart soup pot. Add the potatoes, onion, and parsley. Add the consommé or broth. Bring to a boil and reduce the heat to medium. Cover and continue cooking for 10 minutes, or until the potatoes are tender.

Meanwhile, heat the remaining 1 tablespoon oil, lime juice, basil, and peppercorns in a large skillet over medium heat. When the mixture simmers, add the scallops. Cover and cook for 3 to 4 minutes, until the scallops are just tender; do not overcook. Stir the bread crumbs into the soup pot and cook, uncovered, for 10 minutes. Add the scallops and their liquid to the soup and cook for 2 or 3 minutes more to reheat. Garnish each bowl with a sliver of the fresh lime.

Serves 4–6

Salad

*I*S THERE A BETTER EXAMPLE OF YOUTHFUL FOLLY, someone in the throes of their "salad days," than Peter Rabbit? He just couldn't control himself or his appetite when it came to Mr. McGregor's garden. Peter's problem was that the lure of fresh vegetables overwhelmed his better judgment; he was a true gourmand, not just a naughty little rabbit. We are supposed to think of Peter's random sampling of Mr. McGregor's garden as a cautionary tale, but it's actually quite a nice recipe for a salad: lettuce, French beans, radishes, and parsley.

Leaves always come to mind as the first ingredient in a salad; I am in complete agreement with the rabbit on that. But they might not be the last, and what follows the lettuce into the bowl is entirely up to the imagination and inclination of the cook. Some salads abandon the lettuce altogether and are made of other vegetables, but every salad seems to have plenty of room for a merry hodgepodge of ingredients.

All good greens and vegetables require a saucy send-off on their way to the table: Dressing is the great unifying force in the salad bowl, something to keep Peter Rabbit's enthusiasm in line. There is almost as much variety in the kinds of salad dressings one can make as there are ingredients for salads—and there is an equal amount of variety in possible combinations of dressings and salads. Fresh lettuce with Red Wine Vinegar Dressing is a different dish than the same leaves tossed with Miso Ginger Dressing, and the ease with which one can do this kind of mixing and matching is the key to having a sizable repertoire of salads.

Grains, Dried Beans, and Pasta Salads

MANY SALADS ARE SIDE DISHES that complement the rest of the meal. They can provide a refreshing pause for the diner—a leafy break with a palate-cleansing tang. The more substantial the ingredients in the salad, the more of a meal it becomes. When leaves and vegetables give way to grains, beans, and pasta, the salad can be served as a piquant main course. These dishes make excellent foundations for warm weather dining and vegetarian meals.

Tabbouleh Salad
with Feta Dressing

SEASONING THE BULGUR with a salted vegetable cube is the secret ingredient in this recipe; it makes the bulgur a little less bland and the salad less dependent on the dressing to pull it all together.

¾ cup dried bulgur wheat
1¼ cups boiling water
¾ vegetable bouillon cube
1 cup diagonally sliced baby zucchini
¾ cup halved cherry tomatoes
¼ cup thinly sliced black olives
¼ cup chopped red bell pepper
¼ cup chopped fresh parsley
   Feta Dressing

In a medium bowl, stir the bulgur and the water together. Crumble in the bouillon cube and mix well. Cover and refrigerate for at least 3 hours, or overnight, so that the liquid is absorbed.

Shortly before assembling the salad, steam the zucchini for 3 to 4 minutes, or until tender.

Fluff the bulgur with a fork. Stir in all the vegetables. Add the dressing and toss gently to coat the salad evenly. Chill and serve.

Serves 6

~ Feta Dressing ~

Delicious with tabbouleh, bean salads, cucumber salads, or a handful of kalamata olives and a bowl of leaves.

½ cup crumbled feta cheese
¼ cup olive oil
5 tablespoons freshly squeezed and strained lemon juice
2 teaspoons chopped fresh mint
1 large garlic clove, pressed
¼ teaspoon kosher salt

Puree all the ingredients in a small food processor or blender. The dressing will keep refrigerated for up to 1 week.

Makes about 1 cup

Wild Rice Salad
with Walnut Oil and Lemon Dressing

If THE RICE AND PEAS are warm when they are added, the dressing will permeate the
ingredients and enhance the flavor of the salad. To cook wild rice requires patience;
it always takes a little longer than you think it should. Each grain must "pop" or be
on the verge of popping before the rice is removed from the heat.

¼ cup uncooked wild rice

⅓ cup uncooked brown short-grain rice

1 cup water

1 cup fresh shelled or frozen baby peas

½ cup coarsely chopped pistachio nuts

2 tablespoons chopped fresh parsley

2 tablespoons chopped fresh dill

1 tablespoon chopped fresh chives
   Walnut Oil and Lemon Dressing
   (opposite)

Rinse the wild rice thoroughly under running water. Cover with about 1 inch of water in a medium saucepan. Bring to a boil and cook, uncovered, over medium heat for 15 minutes. Cover and remove from the heat. Set aside for 15 minutes. Drain the wild rice, rinse, and cover with water again. Cook over medium heat, uncovered, replenishing the water as necessary, until tender, about 30 minutes. You should have about 1 cup cooked wild rice.

Meanwhile, combine the brown rice and the water in a small saucepan. Bring to a boil, cover, and reduce the heat to low. Cook until the water has been absorbed, about 30 minutes. Set aside for 10 minutes. You should have 1 cup cooked brown rice. Cook the peas until just tender, about 5 minutes. Immediately remove from the heat and drain.

Mix the wild rice, brown rice, peas, nuts, and herbs together in a medium bowl. Add the dressing and gently toss the salad. Chill before serving.

Serves 4

Ladle, Leaf, & Loaf

~ Walnut Oil and Lemon Dressing ~

Walnut oil is light but rich tasting, and it is very compatible with the freshness of lemon juice. This is a great dressing for salads that do not contain a lot of strongly flavored ingredients, such as onions. Walnut oil can be found in gourmet stores and health food stores.

2 tablespoons walnut oil
2 tablespoons freshly squeezed and strained lemon juice
2 tablespoon water
½ teaspoon kosher salt
Freshly ground black pepper

Combine all the ingredients in a small, tightly lidded jar. Shake well. The dressing will keep refrigerated for up to 1 week.

Makes about ½ cup

THE CULINARY MANTRA about salad dressings says, To do it right, one needs to be "a miser with vinegar, a spendthrift with oil, a counselor with salt, and a madman to shake it all up." A friend from my college days in Berkeley certainly earned "madman" points for tossing a salad by shaking the ingredients, dressing included, in a brown paper bag and then unceremoniously dumping it into a bowl. I was impressed by her free spirit, although at the time neither of us had progressed much beyond iceberg lettuce and bottled dressing. Many meals later, I finally encountered a great salad, and everything fell into place. I guess that's how mantras work. One day, you just get it.

In a well-made salad dressing, the job of the vinegar is to awaken the palate, then it's up to the oil to get the message across. It's important not to overdo it because the dressing has to work with the ingredients of the salad, not overwhelm them. This principle of cooperation between the vinegar and oil applies to all kinds of salad dressings. There are always some ingredients designated to stimulate the palate, such as lemon juice, horseradish, and mustard, and others for spreading the news throughout the salad bowl, like yogurt and buttermilk.

Kosher salt and freshly ground black pepper are obvious essentials in the mix, whereas the addition of garlic and herbs depends on the effect the cook is trying to create. A good salad dressing can liven up the unassuming white bean, flatter an artichoke, and enhance the succulence of tender greens.

Ladle, Leaf, & Loaf

Pasta Salad with Baby Vegetables

Serve this salad in a wide, shallow pasta bowl to display the colorful ingredients.

1 cup shelled fresh or frozen baby peas

1 cup diagonally sliced baby zucchini
  (6–8 whole baby zucchini)

1 cup (about ¼ pound) trimmed baby
  green beans or small, tender green
  beans, cut into ½-inch pieces

12–14 baby carrots, cut lengthwise
  in quarters

½ cup thinly sliced radishes

3 tablespoons chopped fresh flat-leaf
  parsley leaves

1 tablespoon minced fresh chives

½ tablespoon chopped fresh tarragon

½ tablespoon chopped fresh basil

2 tablespoons small capers
  White Balsamic Vinaigrette (opposite)

6 ounces bow-tie pasta (about ½ box)

Cook the peas until just tender, about 5 minutes. Meanwhile, steam the zucchini, beans, and carrots together for 3 to 4 minutes, until just tender. Immediately remove from the heat and drain. Mix all of the cooked vegetables together, including the peas, in a large bowl. Add the radishes, herbs, and capers. Stir in the vinaigrette and set aside.

Fill a large pot with water, bring to a boil, and cook the pasta for 10 to 13 minutes, or until tender. Drain and toss with the vegetables. Cool the salad to room temperature, cover, and refrigerate until thoroughly chilled. Serve cold.

Serves 4–6

~ White Balsamic Vinaigrette ~

A little lighter, sweeter, and more acetic than regular balsamic vinegar, white balsamic vinegar makes a tart, fresh vinaigrette.

- 5 tablespoons olive oil
- 3 tablespoons white balsamic vinegar
- 1 large garlic clove, pressed
- ¼ teaspoon kosher salt, to taste
  Freshly ground black pepper

Combine all the ingredients in a small, tightly lidded jar. Shake well. The dressing will keep refrigerated for up to 1 week.

Makes about ½ cup

BABY VEGETABLES ARE CHARMING—and like all babies, they're irresistible. But we're not dealing with doll food; those adorable teeny summer squashes and itty-bitty green beans are truly delicious. There seems to be some equation at work here: The intensity of flavor is in inverse proportion to size when it comes to these tender morsels. A golf ball–sized beet is far sweeter and has a more concentrated beet flavor then its elders. Young lettuce leaves melt in your mouth, and baby peas are the edible manifestations of spring. I confess I was quite taken in by baby-cut carrots until it dawned on me that unless some ruthless growers were robbing nurseries, those baby carrots must be coming from mature carrots. I still like them though, imposters that they are. These infant vegetables have a brief shelf life. They cost more per pound than the grown-ups. And because they're not commonplace, a little fuss and perhaps a little self-indulgence on the part of the cook is in order.

Green Lentil Salad
with Lemon Dressing

LENTILS MIXED WITH south-of-the-border ingredients and tossed with
lemon dressing make a great main course for a summer meal.

¼ cup green lentils, sorted and rinsed

1 small red bell pepper, chopped

1 small green bell pepper, chopped

½ cup thinly sliced Vidalia onion

1 small avocado, cut into ½-inch chunks

¼–½ cup halved pitted black olives

2 tablespoons chopped fresh cilantro

2 tablespoons chopped fresh chives

Lemon Dressing

Cover the lentils with water in a medium saucepan. Bring to a boil, reduce the heat to low, cover, and cook until the lentils are soft, approximately 40 minutes. Remove from the heat, open the lid slightly, and set aside to cool.

Drain the lentils. In a medium bowl, toss them gently with the peppers, onion, avocado, olives, and herbs. Add the dressing and toss again to coat the ingredients. Refrigerate for 1 hour before serving.

Serves 6

~ Lemon Dressing ~

A very zippy dressing with an intense lemon flavor; try it with beet and carrot salads too.

¼ teaspoon grated lemon rind

¼ cup freshly squeezed and strained
    lemon juice

¼ cup canola oil

1 large garlic clove, pressed

¼ teaspoon kosher salt, or to taste

¼ teaspoon freshly ground black pepper

Combine the ingredients in a small, tightly lidded jar. Shake well. The dressing will keep refrigerated for up to 1 week.

Makes about ½ cup

Ⓣ DIDN'T APPRECIATE BLACK PEPPER until I ate steak tartare in a restaurant in Avignon near the papal palace, where an exhibition of Picasso's final paintings was being held. The dinner and the exhibit were quite an introduction to new ways of experiencing the meanings of the words "raw" and "provocative."

Eating steak tartare was definitely a step beyond sampling cookie dough and cake batter, which had been my only raw food experiences to date, but I was ready to be dazzled and didn't want to miss any opportunity for eating French food on French soil. The tartare looked as if it could turn into my mother's meat loaf if the chef had kept going. More significant for my evolving taste buds, this was the first time I'd ever intentionally bitten into a large piece of a peppercorn. It was like a savory Atomic Fireball jawbreaker, with layers and layers of heat and flavor. I had no idea pepper could be so exciting or so subtle.

I felt just about as daring sneaking a tiny camera into the Picasso exhibit—where cameras were expressly prohibited—and taking black-and-white photographs of the brooding paintings. They were hung in chronological order, one canvas after another—a series of death masks dominated by staring eyes and filling each room with increasing intensity as you drew closer to the last painting. It was an intimate view of Picasso looking directly into his own eyes, which reflected back to him, and to us, his approaching death and his passion for life.

I bought a catalog of the exhibit, but it missed the emotional juxtaposition of the artwork's fire against the cool, gray, Gothic architecture that my photographs caught. I also bought a pepper mill before I left Avignon. It's never failed to deliver the goods: coarsely ground black pepper, big, eye-opening pieces that wake me up.

Ladle, Leaf, & Loaf

White Bean Salad
with Pink Peppercorn Dressing

MILD WHITE BEANS and carrots shift from "ho-hum" to "haute cuisine" when they are seasoned with this dressing.

---

1 cup dried navy beans or cannellini
  beans, sorted and rinsed

1 large carrot, peeled, cut in half lengthwise and sliced on the diagonal
  (about 1 cup)

¼ cup chopped fresh flat-leaf parsley
  Pink Peppercorn Dressing

In a medium saucepan, cover the beans with about 1 inch of water and bring to a boil. Remove from the heat, cover, and set aside for 1 hour. Drain, replenish the water, cover, and cook the beans over medium heat until tender, approximately 1 hour.

Steam the carrots for 5 minutes, or until tender, and drain. Drain the beans. In a medium bowl, mix together the warm beans, carrots, and parsley. Toss with the dressing. Serve the salad at room temperature or chilled.

Serves 4–6

~ Pink Peppercorn Dressing ~

This dressing is like waving a magic wand over a salad; it adds glamour to modest ingredients and brings out the best in them.

¼ cup olive oil

3 tablespoons white wine vinegar

2 garlic cloves, pressed

½ teaspoon kosher salt, or to taste

1 teaspoon crushed pink peppercorns

Combine all the ingredients in a small, tightly lidded jar. Shake well. To enhance the flavors, allow the dressing to sit for several hours. It will keep refrigerated for up to 1 week.

Makes about ½ cup

Ladle, Leaf, & Loaf

Oceanic Salads

I ONCE HAD THE PLEASURE of dining in Venice. I ordered a dish called *mare misto,* which I knew had something to do with the sea. I was not expecting the oceanic sampler that was set down in front of me, and I spent a few minutes looking it over, giving the miniature octopus special consideration. I ate it, along with every other morsel on the plate, and left the table a changed woman. I had learned at one sitting what the sea tastes like. These salads were inspired by my Venetian epiphany.

Mussel Salad
with Poppy Seed Dressing

THIS MIGHT JUST BE MY FAVORITE salad recipe because it hits all the high spots:
It's got looks, taste, style, and substance, and it's easy to make! Serve as a main course with
Crusty Whole Wheat Bread (page 199) and Anchovy Butter (page 250).

---

2   cups dry vermouth

½   teaspoon grated lemon rind

1   tablespoon freshly squeezed and
     strained lemon juice

2   garlic cloves, sliced

2   pounds live mussels, debearded
     and cleaned

    Mixed salad greens for 4
     (about 3 cups)

6   small red-skinned potatoes, boiled,
     peeled, and cut into bite-sized pieces

4   large hard-boiled eggs, peeled

    Poppy Seed Dressing (opposite)

    Crisp Julienned Potatoes (page 54)

In a large skillet, heat the vermouth with the
lemon rind, lemon juice, and garlic until it simmers. Add the mussels. Cover and cook for
approximately 5 minutes, until the mussels open.
Remove from the heat.

Arrange the greens in 4 individual salad bowls.
Sprinkle the potatoes evenly over the greens. Add
1 egg, cut in half lengthwise, to each salad. Drain
the mussels, remove them from their shells, and
distribute them evenly among the salads. Cover
with foil and refrigerate until well chilled. Spoon
the dressing over each salad, garnish with the crisp
potatoes, and serve.

Serves 4

~ Poppy Seed Dressing ~

This delicate dressing is well suited for shellfish, cucumber, and carrot salads, as well as for those made with tender greens.

¼ cup canola oil
¾ teaspoon grated lemon rind
3 tablespoons freshly squeezed and strained lemon juice
½ teaspoon honey
1 tablespoon poppy seeds
¼ teaspoon kosher salt

Combine the oil, lemon rind and juice, and honey in a small, tightly lidded jar. Shake well. Add the poppy seeds and salt. Shake again until thoroughly blended. The dressing will keep refrigerated for up to 1 week.

Makes about ½ cup

Seaweed Salad with Shrimp and Miso Ginger Dressing

THIS SALAD WAS INSPIRED by Japanese cuisine, but the combination of ingredients is the result of a certain amount of artistic license on my part.

½ cup crumbled dried wakame seaweed

½ cup crumbled dried red dulse

4 tablespoons dried hijiki seaweed

½ cup dry vermouth

4 crushed black peppercorns

½ pound medium shrimp, peeled and deveined

½ cup small cubes of firm tofu

¾ cup Steamed Julienned Carrots (page 149)

Miso Ginger Dressing (opposite)

To reconstitute the seaweed, place the wakame, dulse, and hijiki in separate bowls. Cover with boiling water and set aside to soak for 15 minutes, or until tender. Drain and rinse the wakame and dulse; set aside in a sieve. Drain and rinse the hijiki and cover with boiling water. Let sit for an additional 10 minutes, or until tender.

Pour the vermouth into a small skillet, sprinkle with the crushed peppercorns, and heat until the vermouth simmers. Add the shrimp. Cook the shrimp, turning them over as they cook, until they are pink, 3 to 5 minutes. Remove from the heat, drain, transfer to a plate, and set aside to cool.

Drain the hijiki. In a medium bowl, gently mix together all the seaweed, shrimp, tofu, and carrots. Chill thoroughly. Toss with the dressing and serve.

Serves 4–6

~ Miso Ginger Dressing ~

A great all-purpose dressing that works just as well with leafy salad greens as it does with seaweed.

2   tablespoons rice wine vinegar
1   tablespoon miso paste
3   tablespoons peanut oil
¼   teaspoon freshly grated ginger
¼   teaspoon kosher salt

Combine the vinegar and miso in a small, tightly lidded jar. Shake well. Add the remaining ingredients and shake until thoroughly blended. The dressing will keep refrigerated for up to 1 week.

Makes about ½ cup

❧ LESS IS MORE ❧

How to keep shrimp from turning into rubber,
or a brief lesson in the art of understatement in the kitchen

COLOR IS OFTEN THE KEY to knowing when certain foods are properly cooked. You can always poke something with a fork, but when tenderness is the goal and timing is the defining factor, there is no substitute for a good visual benchmark. The unmistakable new green of young shoots and leaves, the glowing backlit orange of carrots and squash, and the tender pink of perfectly cooked shrimp all have a visual appeal that cries, "Eat me!" The right amount of heat and moisture and a good eye are all that's required. Halting the cooking process by removing a pan from the heat or plunging vegetables into cold water will help preserve the fresh texture and flavor of the vegetables and the tenderness of the shrimp. Trust your instincts; your palate will be grateful.

Shrimp Salad with Wilted Lettuce and Balsamic Vinaigrette

I WAS SURPRISED TO DISCOVER how much there is to romaine lettuce when it is heated until it wilts; it behaves more like cabbage than spinach and tastes delicious bathed in Balsamic Vinegar Dressing, basking in the company of all the shrimp. This salad was inspired by one of those close encounters with interesting food in a restaurant.

⅓ cup freshly squeezed and strained lemon juice

1 tablespoon olive oil

4 crushed black peppercorns

1 garlic clove, pressed

½ pound medium shrimp, peeled and deveined

1 head romaine lettuce, leaves washed, separated, and cut in half

2 tablespoons minced fresh chives
   Balsamic Vinaigrette (page 134)

In a medium skillet, heat the lemon juice, oil, peppercorns, and garlic. When the mixture starts to simmer, add the shrimp. Cook, turning the shrimp over as they cook, until they are pink, 3 to 5 minutes. Remove from the heat, drain, transfer to a plate, and set aside to cool.

Steam the lettuce for 3 to 5 minutes, until it wilts. Remove from the steamer, drain, and transfer to a medium bowl. Add the shrimp, sprinkle with the chives, and toss with the dressing. Chill before serving.

Serves 4

~ Balsamic Vinaigrette ~

A no-frills basic dressing that lets the oil and vinegar do the talking.

5   tablespoons olive oil
5   tablespoons balsamic vinegar
1   large garlic clove, pressed
¼   teaspoon kosher salt, or to taste
    Freshly ground black pepper

Combine the ingredients in a small, tightly lidded jar. Shake well.
The dressing will keep refrigerated for up to 1 week.

Makes about ½ cup

Ladle, Leaf, & Loaf

Cucumber Salads

F EVER A VEGETABLE was ruled by the watery sign of the moon, it's the cucumber. As a child helping my mother, I was assigned the job of preparing cukes for salads. The best part was scoring them with a fork, getting spritzed with the cool juice, and making piles of slices that looked like thin, wet gears. Later, when I was working in a busy vegetarian restaurant, someone cut off the end of a cucumber and pressed it onto my forehead, right between my eyes.

It had a pleasant calming effect. Although it looks ridiculous, like the caste mark of some New Age cook, it's since become a habit of mine to wear the end of a cucumber over my "third eye" when I'm puttering around the kitchen making salad.

If I'm going to be cool, I may as well do it right.

Cucumber Salad
with Creamy Garlic Dressing

A SIMPLE, ATTRACTIVE SALAD that demonstrates good looks and good tastes
is often two sides of the same coin when it comes to cooking.

---

1 English cucumber, halved lengthwise
and thinly sliced (about 2½ cups)

1 cup sliced small white button
mushrooms

⅓ cup halved pitted black olives

¼ cup chopped fresh parsley
Creamy Garlic Dressing

In a medium bowl, mix the cucumbers with
the mushrooms, olives, and parsley. Add the
dressing and toss gently. Serve immediately,
or refrigerate before serving.

Serves 4–6

~ Creamy Garlic Dressing ~

This dressing goes well with cucumbers
and also with chicken or potato salads.

⅓ cup nonfat buttermilk

3 tablespoons canola oil

1½ tablespoons Plain Yogurt Cheese
(page 41) or sour cream

2 large garlic cloves, pressed

½ tablespoon minced fresh dill

¼ teaspoon kosher salt

¼ teaspoon ground coriander

Combine all the ingredients in a small, tightly
lidded jar. Shake well. The dressing will keep
refrigerated for up to 1 week.

Makes about ⅔ cup

English Cucumber and Onion Salad with Buttermilk Dressing

SERVE AS A SIDE DISH with Chilled Beet Soup with Beet Greens (page 96) and Potato-Onion Rye Bread (page 202). Or just heap a spoonful of the salad right on the bread as my Eastern European grandmother used to do: it's delicious.

1 English cucumber, thinly sliced or julienned (about 2½ cups)
¾ cup thinly sliced Vidalia onion
Buttermilk Dressing

In a medium bowl, toss the cucumber with the onion. Add the dressing and mix gently to coat the vegetables. Chill thoroughly. Stir before serving.

Serves 4–6

~ Buttermilk Dressing ~

This aromatic dressing is ideal for cucumber salads. It's rich and creamy and doesn't become watery if the salad is dressed and refrigerated before serving.

½ cup nonfat buttermilk
2 teaspoons sugar
¼ teaspoon kosher salt, or to taste
¼ teaspoon caraway seeds
½ cup Plain Yogurt Cheese (page 41)

In a small bowl, mix together the buttermilk, sugar, salt, and caraway seeds. Add the yogurt cheese and stir until well blended. The dressing will keep refrigerated for up to 1 week.

Makes about 1 cup

I HAVE A BONE TO PICK with those packaged fresh herbs that are available in the grocery stores now. It is, of course, a thrill to be able to have fresh thyme in January or fresh basil in February when before, basil in February was just a picture in a gardening catalog that made you long for spring. But how much of those packaged herbs can any sane person

use at once? Rosemary is particularly troubling. A pinch here, a few leaves there, and then what? Basil is worse, tender soul that it is. So perishable!

A friend of mine put the matter in perspective when she declared that such off-season bounty belongs in the "splurge" category. She buys the fresh herbs for special dishes during the winter and dries or freezes the rest. Usually, though, she exercises restraint, waiting for the summer months, when she can pluck herbs fresh from her garden. For those of us without a garden, there are always herbs in pots on the windowsill; being hardy and forgiving species, herbs will grow for almost anyone—even during the winter.

In spite of my friend's practicality, I am still seduced by the promise of those store-bought herbs. I suppose the use-it-or-lose-it rule applies in this case. If a succulent tub of basil is just too irresistible to pass up on a dark winter day, why not just give in and make pesto? Camus might not have been thinking about food when he said, "In the depths of winter, I suddenly discovered within myself an invincible summer," but his observation applies.

Radish and Cucumber Salad
with Green Herb Dressing

Hot RADISHES AND COOL CUCUMBERS in a dressing packed with fresh green herbs—
the perfect simple salad for warm summer days.

1½ cucumbers, peeled, halved lengthwise,
   seeded, and sliced (about 2 cups)
¾ cup sliced radishes
2 scallions, trimmed and thinly sliced
   Green Herb Dressing

Mix the vegetables together in a medium bowl.
Cover and refrigerate until thoroughly chilled. Toss
with the dressing and serve.

Serves 4–6

~ Green Herb Dressing ~

The generous amount of herbs adds a rich
presence to vegetables or pasta salads.

1 garlic clove, pressed
4–5 medium fresh basil leaves, chopped
2 tablespoons minced fresh chives

1 heaping tablespoon fresh parsley leaves
1 tablespoon chopped fresh dill
1 teaspoon chopped fresh tarragon leaves
¼ cup olive oil
3 tablespoons white wine vinegar
2 tablespoons Plain Yogurt Cheese
   (page 41)
¼ teaspoon kosher salt

Combine the garlic and herbs in a small food
processor or blender and blend thoroughly. Add
the oil, white wine vinegar, and yogurt cheese one
at a time, mixing after each addition. Add the salt.
Transfer the dressing to a small, tightly lidded jar
and refrigerate. Shake well before using. The dressing will keep in the refrigerator for up to 1 week.

Makes about ½ cup

Root Vegetable Salads

ROOT VEGETABLES ARE GREAT candidates for marinades. Just after they're cooked, gently toss them with the marinade; as they cool, their flavors will merge and become something far greater than the sum of all the parts. This is most evident in the case of rutabaga. All it takes is some skillful maneuvering with large knives to whittle the vegetable into bite-sized pieces, a steam bath, and a great dressing to transform this peasant into a princess.

Baby Beet Salad
with Horseradish Dressing

BABY BEETS are in their glory tossed with red onions and horseradish dressing.

**10–12 baby beets, about the size of golf balls,
  trimmed and scrubbed**

¼ cup minced red onion
  Horseradish Dressing (opposite)

Cover the beets with water in a medium saucepan and bring to a boil. Reduce the heat to low and cook, uncovered, until tender, about 25 minutes. Remove from the heat and drain. Run cold water over the beets and slip off the skins.

Cut the beets in half and slice. Mix with the onion in a medium bowl. Add the dressing, toss, and chill thoroughly. Stir and serve.

Serves 4–6

~ Horseradish Dressing ~

I've witnessed the power of horseradish on more than one occasion, and seen mighty contestants fall during a spontaneous matzo and horseradish-eating contest at a seder. One participant insisted that white horseradish was hotter than horseradish colored with beet juice, and the other felt the opposite was true. To prove their points, they both ate a tablespoon of each kind on a small square of matzo. Forget about the color—it was eat it and weep! This salad dressing provides a delicious, biting contrast to the flavors of young beets and other root vegetables, proving that, in the right company, horseradish can be brought under control.

¼ cup Plain Yogurt Cheese (page 41)
¼ cup plain nonfat yogurt
2 tablespoons prepared horseradish
2 tablespoons freshly squeezed and strained lemon juice
½ teaspoon kosher salt, or to taste
½ tablespoon prepared mustard

In a small bowl, mix the yogurt cheese and yogurt together. Stir in the horseradish, lemon juice, and salt. Add the mustard and blend well. The dressing will keep in the refrigerator for up to 1 week.

Makes about ¾ cup

*W*E TAKE FOR GRANTED the diversity of the onion family, whose edible members are close relations of the flowering lily. Onions are as essential to cooking as pots and pans. There are some recipes for which a particular type of onion is important, but there are many others for which the generic onion, meaning the ubiquitous yellow variety, is all that's required. Regardless of variety, onions can always be counted on to do their part in a recipe and do it well.

Leeks are the aristocrats of the clan when it comes to soup. They've got all of the flavor and none of the sharpness of their bulbous cousins. Scallions are hot and succulent, excellent ingredients for condiments and garnishes. But my personal favorite is chives. Those tender hollow shoots seem to be the universal herb for all dishes, and nibbling on a fresh chive from the garden is the best sales pitch for onion greens I know of.

Last on the family tree, but most assuredly not least, are shallots and garlic. Shallots can pack a wallop and must be used with some self-control. Like capons—not quite a rooster, not quite a hen—shal-

lots are not exactly onions and are not garlic, either. Elephant garlic
seems to be on the same page with shallots, in a little niche set aside
for the eccentric relatives in the onion family. But regular garlic stands
out there, front and center, with nothing subtle about it and no
apologies for its behavior. I personally don't think there's life without
garlic. If these plants can cause us to weep and reek and still serve as
staples in our larders, they surely must be fundamental to our well-
being. That much about these lilies we can take for granted.

Beet Salad with Capers and Pickled Onions

THIS SALAD is made in layers, and the marinade from the onions flavors the beets as the salad chills. The ingredients are mixed together when the salad is served.

8   baby beets, about the size of golf balls, trimmed and scrubbed

2   tablespoons small capers

2   cups Pickled Onions

Cover the beets with water in a medium saucepan and bring to a boil. Reduce the heat to low and cook, uncovered, until tender, about 25 minutes. Remove from the heat and drain. Run cold water over the beets and slip off the skins.

Cut the beets in half, slice them, and place them in a medium bowl. Sprinkle with the capers. Spoon the pickled onions over the beets and capers. Cover and chill thoroughly. Toss before serving.

Serves 4–6

~ Pickled Onions ~

Terrific with cucumber, bean, and corn salads.

2   cups bite-sized chunks of white onion (2 large)

¼   cup white balsamic vinegar

½   teaspoon honey

1   ¼-inch-square piece of dried red chili

¼   teaspoon kosher salt

1   large bay leaf

¼   teaspoon crushed green peppercorns

Steam the onions until tender, about 5 minutes. In a small bowl, combine the remaining ingredients. Add the onions and stir to coat with the marinade. Cover and set aside at room temperature for 1 hour. Stir occasionally. Refrigerate until ready to serve.

Makes 2 cups

Root Vegetable Salad
with Chive Rice Wine Vinaigrette

THRIFT CAN BE A MUSE in the kitchen: In my restaurant days, with a limited budget
and a lot of imagination, a few hunky rutabagas went a long way at the salad bar.
This recipe is a variation on the old Cosmos Restaurant dish.

1 large carrot, peeled, cut in half
   lengthwise, and sliced on the
   diagonal (about 1 cup)
1 small rutabaga, peeled and cut into
   2-inch strips (about 2½ cups)
1 large yellow onion, quartered
   and sliced
   Chive Rice Wine Vinaigrette

Steam the vegetables together for about 5 minutes, or until tender. Transfer to a medium bowl
and pour the dressing over the hot vegetables.
Cover and cool to room temperature, stirring
occasionally. Refrigerate and chill thoroughly
before serving.

Serves 4

~ Chive Rice Wine Vinaigrette ~

Rice wine vinegar is on the mellower end of
the vinegar spectrum, and it works very well with
the strong flavor of rutabagas and the sweetness of
carrots

5 tablespoons rice wine vinegar
5 tablespoons canola oil
1 garlic clove, pressed
1 tablespoon dried chives
¼ teaspoon kosher salt
   Freshly ground black pepper

Combine all the ingredients in a small, tightly
lidded jar. Shake well. The dressing will keep
refrigerated for up to 1 week.

Makes about ⅔ cup

Root Vegetable Slaw
with Creamy Caraway Dressing

A DEPARTURE FROM THE TRADITIONAL shredded cabbage salad, this trio of root vegetables makes a colorful and tasty slaw tossed with a creamy caraway dressing.

1½ cups julienned peeled carrot
      (1 large carrot)
1½ cups julienned peeled parsnip
      (1 medium parsnip)
1½ cups julienned peeled rutabaga
      (half of a small rutabaga)
      Creamy Caraway Dressing

Steam the vegetables together for 3 to 4 minutes, until just tender. Drain and set aside to cool. Transfer to a medium bowl and toss with the dressing. Cover and chill thoroughly. Stir before serving.

Serves 4–6

~ Creamy Caraway Dressing ~

This dressing also goes well with beet, potato, bean, and cabbage salads.

3 tablespoons nonfat buttermilk
3 tablespoons Plain Yogurt Cheese
   (page 41) or sour cream
2 tablespoons white balsamic vinegar
½ teaspoon caraway seeds
¼ teaspoon kosher salt
¼ teaspoon crushed green peppercorns

Combine all the ingredients in a small, tightly lidded jar. Shake well. The dressing will keep refrigerated for up to 1 week.

Makes about ½ cup

Steamed Carrot Salad
with Ginger Dressing

THIS SWEET AND SPICY salad sprinkled with bits of crystallized ginger makes
a great side dish served with Curried Pumpkin Soup (page 75).

2 cups peeled julienned carrots
    (about 1 large carrot)
½ cup coarsely chopped walnuts
½ cup raisins
    Ginger Dressing
    Slivers of tart apple, such as
    Granny Smith

Steam the carrots, walnuts, and raisins together for 3 to 4 minutes, until the carrots are just tender. Set aside to cool. Transfer to a medium bowl and toss with the dressing. Garnish with the slivers of apple. Serve at room temperature or chilled.

Serves 4

~ Ginger Dressing ~

Sweet, hot, and smooth—the dressing of choice for carrot salads. It's lovely with baby beets, too.

¼ cup freshly squeezed and strained
    lemon juice
¼ cup Plain Yogurt Cheese (page 41)
2 teaspoons honey
1½ tablespoons minced crystallized ginger

Combine the ingredients in a small, tightly lidded jar. Shake well. The dressing will keep refrigerated for up to 1 week.

Makes about ⅔ cup

Hot Potato Salad
with Mustard Dressing

THIS CHEERFUL POTATO SALAD, with its spicy mustard dressing and plenty of fresh chives, is a departure from the standard hot potato salad made with bacon.

---

5 medium red-skinned potatoes, peeled and cut into chunks (about 5 cups)

3 large hard-boiled eggs, peeled and cut into pieces

2 tablespoons minced fresh chives

2 tablespoons diced prepared pimientos
  Freshly ground black pepper
  Mustard Dressing

In a medium saucepan, cover the potatoes with water and bring to a boil. Reduce the heat to low and cook, uncovered, until tender, approximately 20 minutes. Drain. Mix the potatoes with the eggs in a medium bowl. Add the chives, pimientos, and pepper. Toss gently with the dressing and serve.

Serves 4–6

~ Mustard Dressing ~

Simple as can be, this dressing will liven up salads made with greens, potatoes, chicken, and corn.

4½ tablespoons Dijon mustard

4½ tablespoons canola oil

3 tablespoons white wine vinegar
  Kosher salt to taste

Combine all the ingredients in a small, tightly lidded jar. Shake well. The dressing will keep refrigerated for up to 1 week.

Makes about ¾ cup

New Potato Salad
with White Balsamic Vinaigrette

NEW POTATOES need very little in the way of preparation to be at their best.
Some compatible herbs and a light dressing are all that's required
to make a tempting, fresh salad.

2½ **pounds new potatoes, scrubbed**
1 **tablespoon chopped fresh parsley**
1 **tablespoon chopped fresh dill**
1 **tablespoon small capers**
   White Balsamic Vinaigrette (page 121)

Cover the potatoes with water in a medium saucepan and bring to a boil. Reduce the heat to low and cook until tender, about 25 minutes. Drain and set aside. When cool enough to handle, cut into bite-sized pieces.

In a medium bowl, mix together the potatoes, herbs, and capers. Add the dressing and toss gently. Chill thoroughly before serving.

Serves 4–6

Dazzlers

*L*ET'S FACE IT—THERE ARE SALADS, and then there are *salads*. This group of recipes combines interesting ingredients in unusual ways. When you need some fireworks to liven up a meal, any of these will do.

Snow Pea Salad
with Rice Wine Vinaigrette

THIS REFRESHING SALAD was inspired by ingredients from Japanese and Chinese cooking.

4 cups snow peas, trimmed and cut in
   half crosswise (about 1 pound)
2 cups chopped baby bok choy
½ cup peeled and sliced daikon radish
3 scallions, trimmed and thinly sliced
½ cup pea sprouts or radish seed sprouts
   Rice Wine Vinaigrette

Tamari Almonds (page 59)

Steam the snow peas for 2 to 3 minutes, until bright green. Remove from the steamer and immerse immediately in cold water. Drain, transfer to a medium bowl, and cover.

Steam the bok choy for 3 to 4 minutes, until just tender. Remove from the steamer and immerse immediately in cold water. Drain and add to the snow peas, along with the daikon radish, scallions, and sprouts. Chill thoroughly.

Toss with the dressing and serve, garnished with the almonds.

Serves 4–6

~ Rice Wine Vinaigrette ~

This understated sweet and sour dressing also goes nicely with cucumber and fresh bean salads.

3 tablespoons canola oil
¼ cup rice wine vinegar
1 tablespoon white wine vinegar
½ teaspoon kosher salt
¼ teaspoon sugar

Combine all the ingredients in a small, tightly lidded jar. Shake well. The dressing will keep refrigerated for up to 1 week.

Makes about ½ cup

Fiddlehead Salad
with Almond Dressing

FIDDLEHEAD FERNS are a delicacy available only once a year, and for a very short period of time. The fiddleheads must be absolutely fresh and, for best results, rinsed and boiled several times to ensure that they are thoroughly cooked. Tossing the ferns with dressing and marinating them for at least 24 hours before serving provide a dining experience worth waiting for.

Almond Dressing (opposite)
1 cup fresh fiddleheads, brown papery coverings removed
½ cup blanched slivered almonds
⅓ pound fresh arugula, trimmed and well rinsed

Put the dressing in a serving bowl and set aside.

Trim and rinse the fiddleheads. Stir them into a medium saucepan filled with boiling water and cook, uncovered, for 4 minutes. Drain and rinse. Add fresh water to the saucepan and bring to a boil. Stir the fiddleheads into the water and cook for an additional 4 minutes, until they are no longer bright green. Drain and rinse and pat dry with a paper towel.

Put the fiddleheads and almonds in the serving bowl and gently toss with the dressing. Cover and refrigerate until thoroughly chilled; refrigerating for 24 hours will greatly enhance the flavors. When ready to serve, add the arugula and toss with the chilled fiddleheads.

Serves 4–6

~ Almond Dressing ~

Created just for fiddlehead salad, this dressing echoes the delicate nutty flavor of the cooked ferns and adds the flavor of raspberries for an exotic touch.

    3   tablespoons raspberry wine vinegar
    3   tablespoons canola oil
  3–4   drops almond extract
    ¼   teaspoon kosher salt

Combine all the ingredients in a small, tightly lidded jar. Shake well. The dressing will keep refrigerated for up to 1 week.

Makes about ⅓ cup

Roasted Red Pepper Salad

ROASTED PEPPERS can be served not only as a salad but with spreads on bread.
They also make great open-faced sandwiches; try Potato-Onion Rye Bread (page 202)
or French Bread (page 198) slathered with Parmesan Cheese Spread (page 253)
or Green Peppercorn Yogurt Cheese (page 257).

---

3 **large red bell peppers**
Red Wine Vinegar Dressing (opposite)

Roast the peppers: Pierce each one with a long-handled fork and hold it over a gas burner with a medium flame, turning until the skin blackens. If using an electric stove, roast under the broiler 3 to 4 inches from the heat source, turning, until uniformly blackened.

When the skin is completely charred, remove from the heat and place in a small, tightly closed paper bag to steam for about 5 minutes.

Peel the peppers by scraping the skins off gently with a knife. Slice the peppers in half, trim, and remove the seeds and veins. Cut the peppers into strips and transfer to a medium bowl. Pour the warm dressing over the peppers. Serve at room temperature.

Serves 4

Portobello Mushroom Salad
with Red Wine Vinegar Dressing

FRESH GREEN BEANS provide a crisp contrast to the ample portobello mushrooms in this salad; the flavor of the mushrooms is infused with the red wine vinegar dressing.

Red Wine Vinegar Dressing
4   large portobello mushrooms, stems removed, caps rinsed and sliced
2   cups trimmed and diagonally sliced green beans

In a large skillet, heat the dressing. Add the mushrooms and toss gently to coat with the dressing. Cover the pan and cook over medium heat for 10 minutes, or until the mushrooms have begun to soften. Remove from the heat, cover, and set aside.

Steam the beans for 5 minutes, until just tender. Plunge into cold water, drain, and add to the mushrooms. Transfer the salad to a medium bowl. Cover and cool to room temperature. Toss and serve with a slotted spoon.

Serves 6

~ Red Wine Vinegar Dressing ~

Heating the dressing helps it to season salads thoroughly with its savory flavors. Try it with Hot Potato Salad (page 150) or Chicken Salad (page 165).

¼   cup plus 2 tablespoons olive oil
¼   cup red wine vinegar
1   2-inch sprig fresh rosemary
¼   teaspoon kosher salt
    Freshly ground black pepper

Combine all the ingredients in a small saucepan. Simmer over low heat for 3 to 4 minutes. Pour over the vegetables.

Makes about ⅔ cup

Steamed Artichokes
with Garlic and Parsley Dressing

EXCELLENT PICNIC FARE; be sure to bring a loaf of French Bread (page 198) for mopping up the excess dressing, and serve with Gazpacho with Fresh Tarragon (page 89).

---

2 large artichokes

3–4 sprigs fresh marjoram

3–4 sprigs fresh thyme

¼ pound chèvre cheese cut into 4 slices

2 tablespoons small capers

3 tablespoons toasted pine nuts
(page 38)

Garlic and Parsley Dressing
(opposite)

Trim the top leaves of the artichokes, cut off the stems, and rinse the artichokes well under running water. Place about 2 inches of water in a saucepan large enough to hold a vegetable steamer, and put the marjoram and thyme sprigs in the water. Place the steamer in the saucepan, add the artichokes, upside down, cover, and steam for approximately 40 minutes, or until the leaves are tender. Remove from the steamer; set aside to cool.

Cut the cooled artichokes in half lengthwise. Carefully remove the bristly choke with a spoon or a small sharp knife. Arrange the artichoke halves on a plate, cut sides up. Place a medallion of the chèvre in each cavity and sprinkle with the capers and pine nuts. Pour the dressing over the artichokes, cover, and chill thoroughly before serving.

Serves 4

Ladle, Leaf, & Loaf

~ Garlic and Parsley Dressing ~

I prefer lemon juice to vinegar in a dressing for steamed artichokes. The lemon doesn't overwhelm the subtle artichoke flavor and blends perfectly with the garlic.

¼ cup plus 2 tablespoons olive oil
¼ cup freshly squeezed and strained lemon juice
3 small garlic cloves, pressed
½ tablespoon minced fresh parsley
½ teaspoon kosher salt
   Freshly ground black pepper

Combine all the ingredients in a small, tightly lidded jar. Shake well. The dressing will keep refrigerated for up to 1 week.

Makes about ⅔ cup

Goat Cheese Salad with Green Peppercorns

MOST FETA CHEESE is made of cow's milk, but it doesn't have the delicate texture and flavor of feta made from goat's milk. Goat cheese is an acquired taste, but one worth developing. Goat's milk feta is an excellent place to start if you are wary of cheese with the word "goat" attached to it. Some goat's milk feta is made with herbs, and I recommend using it in this recipe if it is available. The dressing is minimal, with just a taste of oil and vinegar and green peppercorns for heat; the feta provides the salt in the salad. Serve with slices of French Bread (page 198).

¼ **pound goat's milk feta cheese, broken into pieces**

½ **cup thinly sliced red bell pepper**

½ **cup coarsely chopped English cucumber**

½ **cup sliced tomatoes**

¼ **cup chopped fresh parsley**

¼ **cup olive oil**

2 **tablespoons white balsamic vinegar**

½ **teaspoon crushed green peppercorns**

Arrange the cheese, red pepper, cucumber, and tomatoes on a serving dish. Sprinkle with the parsley. Combine the remaining ingredients in a small, tightly lidded jar. Shake well and drizzle over the cheese and vegetables.

Serves 4

Ladle, Leaf, & Loaf

Grape and Feta Salad
with Walnut Oil and Raspberry Vinaigrette

I KNEW GRAPES AND FETA CHEESE would be a good combination, but I wasn't prepared to be swept away. This is one of my favorite recipes, and I confess that, for me, one serving is never enough. Chilling the salad greatly enhances the raspberry flavor. Serve with Lemon Quick Bread (page 236) and Chilled Fresh Green Pea Soup (page 91).

3 cups halved seedless red grapes
¾ cup crumbled feta cheese
¾ cup coarsely chopped walnuts
   Walnut Oil and Raspberry Vinaigrette

In a medium bowl, combine the grapes, feta, and walnuts. Toss with the dressing. Refrigerate for several hours before serving.

Serves 4–6

~ Walnut Oil and Raspberry Vinaigrette ~

The delicate flavor of raspberries permeates this dressing, particularly when the salad is refrigerated for several hours until thoroughly chilled.

¼ cup plus 2 tablespoons walnut oil
2 tablespoons raspberry wine vinegar
½ tablespoon honey

Combine the ingredients in a small, tightly lidded jar. Shake well. The dressing will keep refrigerated for up to 1 week.

Makes about ½ cup

WHEN I WAS A TEENAGER, one of my best friends was in her eighties. She was my next-door neighbor's grandmother, and while I admit I had a crush on her handsome grandson, going to visit Granny gave me much more than the occasional glimpse of Prince Charming. Granny was the matriarch of a large extended family, and they lived in a large baronial house with maids, a piano draped with a fringed shawl, a solarium with canaries, and a greenhouse, which is often where I'd find her. She'd be puttering around watering plants, oblivious to the stifling humidity. I thought she was very, very old. I was fascinated with her slightly gauzy outlook, the few missing teeth, and the idea she seemed to have that just about everything in life was amusing, including me. Furthermore, she liked my artwork, which she told me was "cunning" and "quaint."

One afternoon Granny announced that she was going to take me to lunch; I should be ready the next day when she came in a cab to pick me up. After lunch we were going to the art museum. I'd been telling Granny about my favorite contemporary paintings with such enthusiasm that she offered to have a look at them. But first we went to a posh restaurant overlooking a lagoon, where I was introduced to watercress and butter sandwiches with the crusts cut off. I thought they were quite odd, never having eaten little green plants pressed into butter before, not to mention bread with no crusts, and I was intrigued. I remember having to negotiate a lot of silverware and heavy napkins and summoning every ounce of my table manners to get through lunch without a mishap.

At the museum, things went well with the ancient Greeks and Egyptians. The medieval art was a cinch. There was no problem with Rubens, although I thought *The Rape of the Sabine Women* was a bit over the top; Granny breezed through that era unfazed.

When we got to the Impressionist gallery, I hesitated to start with a little Degas depicting the hind ends of race horses, so we parked ourselves on a bench in front of one of Monet's water lilies. Granny was wearing a broad-brimmed straw hat secured with a hat pin, a ruff of lace at her neck fastened with a brooch, and a print dress that covered her almost completely except for her orthopedic shoes. Her outfit was exactly the same shade of purple as Monet's palette. For a while, we just gazed at the huge painting swimming before us. Granny announced to me that she thought Monet was cunning, and she wasn't interested in going any further. I said, "But Picasso is just in the next room." But she was unmoved. Monet was it for her.

I invited Granny to my sixteenth birthday party, and she gamely agreed to come. How she made it down the basement stairs is something to wonder at from this vantage point in my life. But she was a trooper and must have found my friends entertaining. Granny presented me with a package of macaroons and a drawing pad before negotiating the stairs again, leaving a group of gawking teenagers in her wake. My friends couldn't figure out how I'd gotten such a regal and ancient admirer, and I couldn't figure out the significance of her gift. Knowing that her husband had been the president of a railroad, I was hoping for something a bit more lavish. But Granny saw me more clearly than I saw myself at that age; she recognized the importance of art in my life and wanted to encourage me to keep drawing and painting. And what sixteen-year-old doesn't like sweets? What she probably didn't realize was the impact on my palate of those little watercress sandwiches; they awakened a curiosity in me about food that has never wavered.

Ladle, Leaf, & Loaf

Chicken Salad
with Caper Dressing

T HE NEXT TIME you go on a picnic, ditch the mayo and bring along a batch of this chicken salad. It's low in fat and makes a very satisfying main course.

2½ cups bite-sized pieces of cooked chicken

½ cup thinly sliced celery

½ small yellow bell pepper, cut into thin strips

½ cup thinly sliced red onion

1 tablespoon minced fresh chives

Caper Dressing

In a medium bowl, mix the chicken with the vegetables and chives. Toss with the dressing, cover, and chill thoroughly. Stir before serving.

Serves 4–6

~ Caper Dressing ~

T his is a very savory dressing that perks up chicken, bean, and cucumber salads.

½ cup Plain Yogurt Cheese (page 41)

½ cup nonfat yogurt

2 tablespoons white balsamic vinegar

1 large garlic clove, pressed

¼ cup drained large capers

¼ teaspoon kosher salt

¼ teaspoon Hungarian paprika

¼ teaspoon crushed green peppercorns

In a small bowl, blend the yogurt cheese, yogurt, and vinegar. Stir in the garlic and capers. Add the seasonings and mix well. The dressing will keep refrigerated for up to 1 week.

Makes about 1 cup

Summer and Winter Salads

I STUBBORNLY CLING TO THE NOTION that there is still a viable connection between food and the seasons, even though seasonal produce is becoming a concept with very blurry boundaries in the modern grocery store. I don't eat apples in the spring and summer; they've been in storage for months by then and have none of the  appeal that a crisp McIntosh has on a brisk fall day. Serving a fresh bell pepper salad in December seems equally inappropriate. And despite its ubiquitous year-round presence, cabbage salad in midsummer doesn't sound nearly as appetizing to me as Summer Bean Salad with Lime Cilantro Dressing.

Summer Bean Salad
with Lime Cilantro Dressing

Pine nuts add the taste of southwestern cooking to this salad.
The Lime Cilantro Dressing extends the culinary borders a bit farther south
with refreshing results.

---

2 cups green beans, trimmed and
snapped in half (about ½ pound)

2 cups wax beans, trimmed and
snapped in half (about ½ pound)

1 cup fresh corn kernels (1–2 ears)

2 large radishes, thinly sliced

¼ cup toasted pine nuts (page 38)
Lime Cilantro Dressing

Steam the beans for 5 minutes, or until just tender. Mix together the beans, corn, radishes, and pine nuts in a medium bowl. Toss with the dressing. Serve chilled.

Serves 6

~ Lime Cilantro Dressing ~

This dressing behaves like a marinade, steeping the vegetables with flavor while the salad is refrigerated.

¼ cup freshly squeezed and strained
lime juice

5 tablespoons canola oil

1 garlic clove, pressed

2 tablespoons minced fresh cilantro

⅛ teaspoon salt

Combine all the ingredients in a small, tightly lidded jar. Shake well. The dressing will keep refrigerated for up to 1 week.

Makes about ½ cup

Fresh Pepper Salad
with Basil Dressing

FAMILY TIES between vegetables can make dishes that are particularly harmonious, like a group of siblings who sing together. This salad features two of the delicious edible members of the nightshade family—a natural duo.

1 cup chopped red bell pepper
1 cup chopped green bell pepper
1 cup chopped orange bell pepper
½ cup white onion, sliced and cut into
    1-inch strips (about ½ cup)
½ cup grape or cherry tomatoes
   Basil Dressing

Combine all the vegetables in a medium bowl. Toss with the dressing. Serve at room temperature or chilled.

Serves 4–6

~ Basil Dressing ~

This is a good dressing to use if you have guests that are "garlic shy." The white wine vinegar draws the flavor from the minced herb, giving this dressing a pleasing basil taste.

5 tablespoons canola oil
3 tablespoons white wine vinegar
½ teaspoon minced fresh basil
¼ teaspoon kosher salt
   Freshly ground black pepper

Combine the ingredients in a small, tightly lidded jar. Shake well. The dressing will keep refrigerated for up to 1 week.

Makes ½ cup

Corn Salad
with Lime Dressing

THIS SALAD IS RIGHT ON THE BORDER between salad and salsa—
delicious with Posole with Chicken (page 99).

2 cups fresh corn kernels (4–5 ears)
⅓ cup sliced black olives
¼ cup chopped green bell pepper
¼ cup plum tomato
½ large avocado, coarsely chopped
¼ cup chopped radishes
1 tablespoon chopped fresh garlic chives
    or ordinary chives
    Lime Dressing

Combine all the vegetables and chives in a
medium bowl. Toss with the dressing. Serve at
room temperature or chilled.

Serves 4–6

~ Lime Dressing ~

Created just for corn salad, this dressing
bathes the ingredients with an intense lime flavor.

3 tablespoons canola oil
½ teaspoon grated lime rind
2 tablespoons freshly squeezed and
    strained lime juice
¼ teaspoon kosher salt
    Freshly ground black pepper

Combine all the ingredients in a small, tightly
lidded jar. Shake well. The dressing will keep refrigerated for up to 1 week.

Makes about ⅓ cup

Apple and Red Onion Salad
with Honey-Mustard Dressing

THIS SALAD is reminiscent of chutney. It's a mixture of fruit, nuts, and onions with a sweet and spicy dressing. Serve with Curried Pumpkin Soup (page 75) and Corn Sticks (page 219).

---

4 cups bite-sized unpeeled tart apples, such as Granny Smith

1½ tablespoons freshly squeezed and strained lemon juice

½ cup coarsely chopped walnuts

¼ cup red onion, chopped
Honey-Mustard Dressing

Toss the apples with the lemon juice in a medium bowl. Mix in the walnuts and onion, add the dressing, and toss. Serve at room temperature.

Serves 4–6

~ Honey-Mustard Dressing ~

This dressing is proof that in cooking, as in love, opposites attract and can complement each other beautifully.

¼ cup plus 2 tablespoons canola oil

2 tablespoons freshly squeezed and strained lemon juice

2 teaspoons honey

2 teaspoons Dijon mustard

Combine all the ingredients in a small, tightly lidded jar. Shake well. The dressing will keep refrigerated for up to 1 week.

Makes about ½ cup

Cabbage and Apple Salad
with Spicy Peanut Dressing

THE INSPIRATION for this salad was a friend's Japanese noodle dish with spicy Thai peanut sauce. Keeping the cross-cultural ball rolling, I paired her peanut sauce with a cabbage and apple salad, which has German-American roots.

---

2 cups bite-sized pieces of unpeeled tart apples, such as Granny Smith or Cortland

1½ cups thinly sliced savoy cabbage

1½ tablespoons freshly squeezed and strained lemon juice

¼ cup unsalted roasted peanuts
Spicy Peanut Dressing

Mix together the apples and cabbage in a medium bowl. Toss with the lemon juice. Sprinkle with the peanuts. Add the dressing and stir to coat the salad evenly. Serve at room temperature.

Serves 6

~ Spicy Peanut Dressing ~

This is a smooth, rich, spicy dressing with a distinctive peanut flavor.

¼ cup nonfat buttermilk

3 tablespoons unsalted, unsweetened peanut butter

1 tablespoon freshly squeezed and strained lemon juice

½ teaspoon honey

¼ teaspoon kosher salt

1 ½-inch-square piece of dried red chili, minced

In a small bowl, mix together the buttermilk and peanut butter. Blend in the lemon juice and honey. Stir in the salt and chili. The dressing will keep refrigerated for up to 1 week.

Makes about ½ cup

SINCE THE PRESENCE OR ABSENCE of salt alters the flavor of a dish dramatically, its use requires discretion. Too little, and flavors can seem disconnected and the overall effect can be bland. Too much, and the salt overpowers everything else. Of course, as a cook, one aspires to please the greatest number of people by achieving the right balance of ingredients—and that's where kosher salt comes in.

Kosher salt has a presence that plain old table salt just can't muster. At first, I thought the larger crystals were just more elegant—but then I realized that one-quarter teaspoon of kosher salt delivers a different kind of taste than the same quantity of table salt. It tastes less salty, and I find I'm more inclined to use it judiciously because I can sprinkle a few grains into a dish and actually taste the difference. The coarse crystals don't get away from you as table salt does, and that allows for some very desirable fine-tuning.

Cabbage and Black Olive Salad with Garlic Caraway Dressing

SAVOY CABBAGE is the tender member of the cabbage family, refined enough to serve with capers and olives.

3½ cups 1½-inch-wide strips of savoy cabbage

½ cup sliced black olives

¼ cup minced fresh chives

2 tablespoons small capers

Garlic Caraway Dressing

Combine the cabbage, olives, chives, and capers in a medium bowl. Add the dressing and toss. Chill thoroughly and stir before serving.

Serves 4

~ Garlic Caraway Dressing ~

There's nothing subtle about this dressing, with its happy excess of garlic and the unmistakable presence of caraway seeds. It gets right down to business, adding flavor to cabbage, potato, and bean salads.

5 tablespoons olive oil

3 tablespoons white wine vinegar

4 garlic cloves, pressed

½ teaspoon caraway seeds

¼ teaspoon kosher salt

Freshly ground black pepper

Combine all the ingredients in a small, tightly lidded jar. Shake well. The dressing will keep refrigerated for up to 1 week.

Makes about ½ cup

Lettuce Salads

THE FOLLOWING RECIPES are the most humble in the bunch—simple salads of leaves and dressing, with a crouton or nut added on the way to the table. A good fresh salad calls forth the happy herbivore within us, for who can resist tender greens, toothsome, crisp, and cool?

Endive Salad with Roasted Garlic Dressing

ENDIVE HAS ATTITUDE. It's not the kind of salad material that gets shredded or torn and tossed into the salad bowl. Arranging endive leaves on a plate and drizzling them with dressing is the way to treat these strong-flavored, fancy greens.

---

4 small Belgian endives
Roasted Garlic Dressing

Trim and slice the endives in half lengthwise; arrange the leaves on individual plates. Drizzle the dressing over the endive and serve.

Serves 4

~ Roasted Garlic Dressing ~

This is the mellow approach to a salad dressing loaded with garlic. It has lots of flavor without the sharpness of fresh garlic.

6 roasted garlic cloves (page 196)
¼ cup olive oil
2 tablespoons white wine vinegar
¼ teaspoon kosher salt
Freshly ground black pepper

Combine all the ingredients in a small food processor or blender and blend thoroughly. The dressing will keep refrigerated for up to 1 week.

Makes about ⅓ cup

Ladle, Leaf, & Loaf

Belgian Endive and Boston Lettuce Salad with Savory Orange Dressing

ELEGANT GREENS arranged in individual servings, this salad is more for "dining" than eating dinner.

---

4 small Belgian endives
1 head Boston lettuce, rinsed and dried
   Savory Orange Dressing

¼ cup chopped toasted hazelnuts
   (page 38)

Trim and cut the endives in half lengthwise and separate the leaves. Tear the Boston lettuce into bite-sized pieces. Arrange the greens on individual plates. Drizzle the dressing over the greens, and garnish with the hazelnuts.

Serves 4

~ Savory Orange Dressing ~

Try this exotic orange dressing with baby beets as well as with endive salad.

¼ cup canola oil
2 tablespoons orange juice concentrate
1 tablespoon rice wine vinegar
¼ teaspoon grated orange rind
¼ teaspoon Worcestershire sauce

Combine all the ingredients in a small, tightly lidded jar. Shake well. The dressing will keep refrigerated for up to 1 week.

Makes about ⅓ cup

Summer Garden Salad
with Tarragon Vinaigrette

PLUNDER THE LETTUCE PATCH, mix up a batch of mellow Roasted Garlic Dressing or Tarragon Vinaigrette, and add a handful of Herb and Cheese Croutons for a classic salad course.

Fresh garden lettuce for 6, rinsed, dried, and torn into bite-sized pieces (about 3 cups)

Roasted Garlic Dressing (page 175) or Tarragon Vinaigrette

1 cup Herb and Cheese Croutons (page 67)

Arrange the lettuce in individual bowls. Drizzle with dressing, sprinkle with the croutons, and serve.

Serves 6

~ Tarragon Vinaigrette ~

¼ cup olive oil

2½ tablespoons white balsamic vinegar

1 tablespoon minced fresh tarragon

¼ teaspoon kosher salt

Freshly ground black pepper

Combine all the ingredients in a small, tightly lidded jar. Shake well. The dressing will keep refrigerated for up to 1 week.

Makes about ⅓ cup

❧ LEAVES ❧

LETTUCE HAS BROKEN THE BONDS of orthodoxy, arriving in the grocery store in two previously unknown forms: in packaged salads and as the best produce free-for-all ever, inviting heaps of mixed lettuce leaves, with tongs supplied. Prior to this conceptual leap, there wasn't much to choose from in the produce department besides the old standbys: red leaf, green leaf, and iceberg. But whether lettuce is wrapped in cellophane or selected one leaf at a time, it is very perishable.

Lettuce provides one of the clearest examples of the presence of a life force in harvested vegetables. It is still alive when it's been picked and for some time continues to carry on the biological function of respiration. Respiration produces

Ladle, Leaf, & Loaf

heat, and heat removes water from the plant's cells. Refrigerating lettuce slows down this process, keeping those leaves hydrated and crisp. There's a reason for giving lettuce plenty of cold showers in the grocery store. It literally provides life support. When these measures start to fail, the outer leaves wilt and get jettisoned, the stems get trimmed, and it's downhill from there. That's the bad news. But the good news is the same whether it's leaves, stems, flowers, fruits, or roots: The shorter the time and distance from the garden to the table, and the more care taken en route, the better the quality of the food we eat.

Mixed Green Salad
with Red Wine Vinegar Dressing

I PICTURE "FIELD MIX" coming from some kind of vast lettuce land inhabited by endless varieties of young leaves, all living in harmony. Regardless of how they are actually grown, these greens make wonderful salads. Use a light hand with the dressing and croutons so you don't mask the taste of the greens.

Mixed baby greens (also called "field mix") for 6, rinsed and dried (about 9 cups)
Red Wine Vinegar Dressing (page 157)
Garlic Croutons (page 79)

Arrange the greens in individual bowls. Drizzle with the dressing, sprinkle with the croutons, and serve.

Serves 6

Summer Garden Salad
with Tofu Sesame Dressing

GO FOR THE LARGER VARIETIES of lettuce when making this salad;
they are more compatible with heavier dressings like Tofu Sesame.

**Mixed summer salad greens for 6,
rinsed, dried, and torn into bite-sized
pieces (about 9 cups)
Tofu Sesame Dressing
½ cup Tamari Almonds (page 59)**

Put the greens in a salad bowl. Add the
dressing, toss the salad, sprinkle with the almonds,
and serve.

Serves 6

~ Tofu Sesame Dressing ~

This high-protein dressing has a strong
sesame flavor and smooth texture, suitable for leafy
green salads that are served with Lentil Soup with
Hijiki (page 82) or Red Lentil and Kale Soup
(page 84).

**¼ cup firm tofu
2 tablespoons hulled sesame seeds
1 teaspoon tahini (available in health
food stores and some supermarkets)
3 tablespoons rice wine vinegar
1 tablespoon peanut oil
½ teaspoon sesame oil
¼ teaspoon kosher salt**

Blend the tofu in a small food processor or
blender until smooth. Add the sesame seeds and
tahini and pulse the machine to mix. Add the
remaining ingredients and blend well. The dressing
will keep refrigerated for up to 1 week.

Makes about ½ cup dressing

❧ MUSINGS ❧

As I wrote this book, I began to feel as though I inhabited a world bordered by "medium bowls," "small, tightly lidded jars," and "4½-quart soup pots." Repeating these terms in an instruction manual, which, after all, is what a cookbook is, certainly made one thing clear to me: There's a method in the madness!

If you do something over and over again, not only does the process become easier—you also pick up some skills along the way. I experienced this when I raised milk goats. Years of handling different quantities of milk made me a pro at measuring liquids by eye, and although the goats are long gone, I haven't lost my measuring edge in the kitchen. The same situation occurs in the studio, but in a somewhat different way. Every time I make a new piece of artwork, the facility I have with my tools improves, and that gets me closer to

Ladle, Leaf, & Loaf

bringing forth the images I see in my head—just as being familiar with my pots and pans helps me create new recipes.

I'm a whiz with scissors, but I can't direct my muses; I have to take my cue from them. Actually, they're a lot like my goats. I had a 51 to 49 percent partnership with them—they had the 51 percent—and my muses definitely have the upper hand, too. The goats and I had an agreement: I gave them food and shelter in exchange for milk. Art is much harder to negotiate with. It's more difficult to express an idea artistically than it is to coax a stubborn goat up onto a milk stand, although they can be equally frustrating experiences.

When I put on my apron, I always have to confront a certain amount of chaos before dinner ends up on the table, which is the way I feel when I start an art project. Knowing the ingredients and being comfortable with the equipment is like having a compass. I know where I'm starting and where I want to end up; I just have to find out how to get there.

Tossed Green Salad
with Pine Nut Dressing

A SALAD WITH THIS DRESSING would be equally appropriate served with the Italian-style Autumn Vegetable Minestra (page 73) or the Mexican-style Posole with Chicken (page 99).

Salad greens for 6, washed, dried, and torn into bite-sized pieces (about 9 cups)
Pine Nut Dressing
1 **cup Cumin-Chili Croutons (page 93)**
1 **tablespoon pine nuts**

Put the lettuce in a salad bowl. Add the dressing, sprinkle with the croutons and pine nuts, and serve.

Serves 6

~ Pine Nut Dressing ~

All nuts require work to free them from their shells, and pine nuts are among the most difficult to extract; they are small, and the job is labor-intensive, making these nuts expensive.

Fortunately, a little goes a long way—and with just a tablespoon of pine nuts, this recipe makes a dressing rich with their unique flavor.

1 **tablespoon pine nuts**
2 **tablespoons white balsamic vinegar**
3 **tablespoons canola oil**
1 **garlic clove, pressed**
¼ **teaspoon kosher salt**
Freshly ground black pepper

Chop the pine nuts in a small food processor. Add the vinegar and blend well. Add the oil, garlic, salt, and pepper. Pulse the machine to blend thoroughly. The dressing will keep refrigerated for up to 1 week.

Makes about ⅓ cup

Bread

BREAD IS THE ORIGINAL ICON FOR OUR CIVILIZA-
TION, marking the transition our species made from hunting and gathering to settling down and growing crops. It is one of the oldest foods
there is and probably has more metaphorical clout than any other
comestible. We eat it, earn it, and use it to preach values: that man does

not live by bread alone, but half a loaf is better than none, and if you know what side your bread is buttered on, you are in good shape. If Hansel and Gretel's parents had not been willing to sacrifice their children for a scrap of bread, the children would not have been sent into the forest, and there would be no story to tell. How deprived we would be without this literary object lesson about the power of bread! In the fairy tale, bread is food, an expression of affection, a road map, and it is even instrumental in the demise of a wicked witch; the oven Gretel pushed the witch into was supposedly being heated for baking bread.

Having bread or a lack of it is a very serious matter. Marie Antoinette had too much bread, the peasants had too little, and she lost her head by suggesting they eat cake instead. The peasants certainly took matters into their own hands, and the connection between bread and revolution has not been lost on subsequent generations. When I was a student at Berkeley in the sixties, a riot was precipitated by the takeover of a vacant lot the university owned. The perpetrators were students and street people who had turned the eyesore into a benign little park. Suddenly a fence sprang up around the park, making it off limits and a symbol of the

Ladle, Leaf, & Loaf

establishment's nonnegotiable power. One night, loaves of bread were passed among the supporters of People's Park, and inside each loaf was a pair of wire cutters. We had a joyous evening breaking bread together, supping, and snipping.

Most bread is not surrounded by such drama, and no one goes to the grocery store with a list that says "detergent, juice, cat food, staff of life, ice cream . . ." But bread is certainly something we live with on a daily basis—and have for so long that our response to it seems almost instinctual. There is nothing more evocative of hearth and home.

Yeast Breads

UNLIKE THE LITTLE RED HEN, I think making bread is a delightful task, and I don't mind doing it alone. The smell of baking bread is the most powerful pheromone any kitchen emits. If the Little Red Hen had fed the recalcitrant critters fresh bread first and enlisted their help in making the next batch, they probably would have caved in on the spot, signed up for kitchen duty, and squabbled over the credit! Making bread is very simple and satisfying, with only one cardinal rule: Don't kill the yeast! If you can comfortably and briefly hold your finger in the liquid used for dissolving the yeast, then you're home free. Kneading bread is one of the best excuses there is to play in the kitchen, and by doing so, you will learn what the expression "springs back lightly to the touch" really feels like. Punching down bread that has risen is just plain fun—and proof that things are going well; you know the yeast is doing its job. By the time the bread is in the oven, you'll already be looking forward to eating it.

Garlic Breadsticks

THESE BREADSTICKS are slender and crisp, rich with the savory flavor of garlic, and they make a very attractive presentation at the table. My mother-in-law used to say that being "thin, rich, and beautiful" was something to aspire to, and these breadsticks have it all.

1 package dry yeast

1 cup lukewarm water

4 teaspoons olive oil

About 2¼ cups bread flour or all-purpose flour

¼ tablespoon pressed garlic

1 teaspoon kosher salt, plus more for sprinkling

Cornmeal for sprinkling

In a large mixing bowl, dissolve the yeast in the lukewarm water. Stir and let stand until foamy, 3 to 5 minutes. Add 1 teaspoon of the oil and beat in ½ cup of the flour. Set aside.

Heat the remaining 3 teaspoons oil in a small skillet. Stir in the garlic and cook until lightly browned. Cool for 3 to 4 minutes and add it to the flour mixture. Stir in the 1 teaspoon salt. Gradually stir in about 1½ cups flour.

Transfer the dough to a lightly floured surface and knead in the remaining ¼ cup flour, or more as needed, until the dough is smooth and elastic. Put the dough in a lightly buttered medium bowl, grease the surface, cover with a damp cloth, and set aside in a warm place to rise for about 1 hour, or until almost doubled in size.

At least 15 minutes before you bake, preheat the oven to 450 degrees. Sprinkle a baking sheet with the cornmeal and set aside.

Punch down the dough and divide it in half. Roll out each piece into a log about 10 inches long. Cut each log into 8 to 10 pieces. Roll out each piece into a thin, 10-inch "stick" and transfer to the baking sheet about 2 inches apart. Sprinkle with salt. Bake for 10 to 15 minutes, or until lightly browned. Cool on a wire rack before serving.

Makes 16–20 breadsticks

Pine Nut Breadsticks

I WONDER IF I SHOULD have called these "breads" instead of "sticks." Or "breadlets," perhaps? Nomenclature aside, these moist and delicately flavored small members of the bread family make fine fare served with pureed vegetable soups.

¼ teaspoon sugar

½ cup lukewarm water

1 package dry yeast

About 1¼ cups all-purpose flour

½ cup finely ground pine nuts

2 tablespoons canola oil

1¼ teaspoons kosher salt

1 large egg white, beaten

In a large mixing bowl, stir the sugar into the lukewarm water. Add the yeast, stir to dissolve, and let stand until foamy, 3 to 5 minutes. Beat in ½ cup of the flour, the pine nuts, oil, and salt. Gradually add the remaining ¾ cup flour, stirring after each addition.

Transfer the dough to a lightly floured surface and knead, adding more flour as needed, until smooth and elastic. Put the dough in a lightly buttered medium bowl. Grease the surface, cover with a damp cloth, and set aside in a warm place to rise for about 1 hour, or until almost doubled in size.

At least 15 minutes before you bake, preheat the oven to 450 degrees.

Punch down the dough. Roll it into a log about 10 inches long. For each breadstick, pinch off 1 tablespoon of dough from the log. Roll out each piece into a thin, 6-inch stick and transfer to an ungreased baking sheet. Brush with the beaten egg white.

Place a cast-iron skillet on the bottom of the oven. Fill halfway with warm water. Bake the breadsticks for 10 minutes, or until lightly browned. Cool on a wire rack before serving.

Makes 18 breadsticks

Saffron Rolls

SAFFRON-TINTED and tender, these rolls go well with Asparagus Essence with Toasted Almonds (page 37) or Chilled Fresh Green Pea Soup (page 91). An egg, butter, honey, and nutmeg give the rolls a rich flavor.

1¼ cups skim milk
1 tablespoon honey
¼ teaspoon saffron threads
1 package dry yeast
1 large egg
2 tablespoons butter, melted
¾ teaspoon kosher salt
Pinch of nutmeg
About 3¼ cups all-purpose flour

In a small saucepan, scald the milk. Stir in the honey and saffron. Transfer to a large bowl. When the mixture is lukewarm, sprinkle it with the yeast, stirring to dissolve. Let stand until foamy, 3 to 5 minutes.

In a small bowl, beat together the egg, butter, salt, and nutmeg. Add the egg mixture to the milk. Beat in 3 cups of the flour, 1 cup at a time. Transfer the dough to a lightly floured surface and knead until smooth and elastic, using the remaining ¼ cup flour, or more as needed, to prevent the dough from sticking.

Put the dough in a lightly buttered medium bowl. Grease the surface, cover with a damp cloth, and set aside in a warm place to rise for about 1 hour, or until almost doubled.

About 15 minutes before you bake, preheat the oven to 400 degrees. Butter two muffin pans and set aside.

Punch down the dough and divide it into 18 pieces. Roll each piece into a ball and place in a muffin cup, or divide each piece into thirds, roll each little piece into a ball, and place the 3 little balls together in a muffin cup to form a cloverleaf roll. Bake the rolls for 10 to 12 minutes, or until lightly browned. Serve warm.

Makes 18 rolls

A RT AND CUISINE RARELY spring forth from my hands like Athena, fully formed, but that is something to aspire to. I once knew a famous graphic designer whose aesthetic sensibilities were so well developed that she couldn't toss a dishtowel next to the sink without its looking beautiful. She made ratatouille the way she laid out a book, and always ended up with a feast, regardless of whether it was to satisfy the eye or stomach. I've tried to emulate her sense of style, and have been humbled by its deceptive simplicity. It's one thing to understand that the eye should move with ease around a well-conceived piece of artwork, or that the flavors of good food should move smoothly across the palate, and quite another to pull it off. That requires some native ability, plain old-fashioned elbow grease, and, in my case, eternal optimism. Move over, Sisyphus.

I think the artistic temperament is like the urge of a hungry horse to follow a carrot at the end of a stick: relentless and very focused. It's foolish, perhaps, but if I am a fool to try and create beauty in my life, so be it. My inclination is to follow Aphrodite and hand over the apple to her; I'm with Paris on that one.

Making art is a decidedly nonlinear experience for me. Sometimes I feel as though I am out there with Odysseus, lashed to the mast trying

to get past the Sirens, or worse, caught between my own version of Scylla and Charybdis, devoid of inspiration. Odysseus had Athena's guidance to get him through, and while I can't claim such an ally, I fall back on the advice of a kayaking teacher I once had—when you are faced with the rapids, paddle like hell! It's messy but effective; wisdom and power don't have to look good to work well in a pinch. They're just not so great as icons of artistic expression. That's Aphrodite's domain.

When Aphrodite gave Psyche a huge pile of mixed seeds to sort and a deadline that was impossible to meet, the lowly ants came to Psyche's rescue. They moved the seeds into separate piles and made order out of chaos. It was Psyche's lesson in the rewards of perseverance, discrimination, and patience. Aphrodite was a tough mother-in-law-to-be, but it turned out well in the end. Psyche got her man back—she just had to work hard to make it happen. It's a big job to unite Love with the Soul when Beauty is such a demanding mistress, and I guess you get there incrementally—one grain, and one toss, at a time.

Pita Breads

BEING FULL of hot air is something none of us would like to be accused of; it works just fine, however, in pita breads, because hot air is what creates the pocket inside the bread.

---

1 teaspoon honey

1 cup lukewarm water

1 package dry yeast

½ cup chickpea flour

1 teaspoon kosher salt

¼ teaspoon paprika

   About 1½ cups plus 2 tablespoons bread flour or all-purpose flour

   Cornmeal for sprinkling

In a large mixing bowl, stir the honey into the water. Add the yeast and stir to dissolve. Let stand until foamy, 3 to 5 minutes. Mix in the chickpea flour, salt, and paprika. Beat in 1 cup of the flour. Gradually add another ½ cup of the flour. Transfer the dough to a lightly floured surface. Knead until smooth and elastic, using the remaining 2 tablespoons bread flour, or more as needed, to prevent the dough from sticking.

Put the dough in a lightly buttered medium bowl. Grease the surface, cover with a damp cloth, and set aside in a warm place to rise for about 1 hour, or until almost doubled.

Punch down the dough and divide it into 6 pieces. Roll each piece into a ball. Cover with plastic wrap and let rest for 15 minutes. Meanwhile, at least 15 minutes before you bake, preheat the oven to 450 degrees. Sprinkle a baking sheet with the cornmeal and set aside.

Roll each ball into a circle about 5 to 7 inches wide with a rolling pin. Transfer the rounds to the baking sheet, 3 inches apart.

Bake the breads for 8 to 10 minutes, or until they puff up and brown. Remove from the oven and immediately wrap in clean towels for 15 minutes to prevent the pitas from deflating and drying out. Serve warm.

Makes 6 pitas

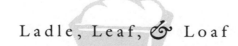

Anise Bread

Here's a sweet, fragrant bread flavored with oranges and anise that makes great toast. Serve with Golden Lemon Chicken Soup (page 102) and Summer Garden Salad with Tarragon Vinaigrette (page 177).

---

1 cup skim milk

¼ cup orange juice

2 tablespoons honey

1 package dry yeast

1 large egg

1 tablespoon unsalted butter, melted

1 tablespoon anise seed

1 teaspoon kosher salt

½ teaspoon grated orange rind

½ teaspoon ground cinnamon

About 3⅔ cups all-purpose flour

In a small saucepan, heat the milk, orange juice, and honey. Pour into a large mixing bowl and cool to lukewarm. Add the yeast, stirring to dissolve. Let stand until foamy, 3 to 5 minutes. Beat the egg and butter together in a small bowl and add to the yeast mixture. Stir in the anise, salt, orange rind, and cinnamon.

Gradually add 3 cups of the flour, beating after each addition. Transfer the dough to a lightly floured surface and knead in the remaining ⅔ cup flour, or more as needed, until the dough is smooth and elastic.

Put the dough in a lightly buttered medium bowl. Grease the surface, cover with a damp cloth, and set aside in a warm place to rise for about 1 hour, or until almost doubled. Lightly oil two 8½-x-4½-inch loaf pans with vegetable spray and set aside.

Punch down the dough and form 2 loaves. Transfer to the baking pans and let rise for an additional 20 minutes. Meanwhile, preheat the oven to 375 degrees.

Bake the loaves for 40 minutes, or until the bread makes a hollow sound when tapped. Cool thoroughly on a wire rack before slicing.

Makes 2 loaves

Forty-Clove Garlic Bread

BAKING GARLIC changes it from a flavoring agent to a vegetable that is delicious spread
on French bread; blending the cooked garlic right into the bread seemed like the logical next step.
A rubber garlic peeler (see page 25) is highly recommended for this recipe. If you're really mad
about garlic, slice the loaf, brush the slices with chopped garlic sautéed in melted butter
or in equal amounts of melted butter and olive oil, wrap the loaf in foil,
heat in the oven, and live it up!

---

40 garlic cloves, peeled (4–5 bulbs)
1 tablespoon olive oil
1 package dry yeast
1¼ cups lukewarm water
   About 3 cups bread flour or
   all-purpose flour
½ tablespoon kosher salt

To roast the garlic: Preheat the oven to 400 degrees. Place the garlic cloves on a piece of aluminum foil large enough to fold over the cloves and seal. Drizzle the oil over the garlic, cover with the foil, and seal. Bake for about 40 minutes, or until tender. When cool enough to handle, put the cloves in a small bowl, mash with a fork, and set aside.

In a large mixing bowl, dissolve the yeast in the water. Stir and let stand until foamy, 3 to 5 minutes. Stir in 1 cup of the flour and blend well. Mix in the salt and mashed garlic. Gradually add the remaining 2 cups flour, stirring after each addition. Transfer the dough to a lightly floured surface and knead until smooth and elastic. Use additional flour, if necessary, to prevent the dough from sticking.

Put the dough in a lightly buttered medium bowl. Grease the surface, cover with a damp cloth, and set aside in a warm place to rise for about 1 hour, or until almost doubled.

At least 15 minutes before you bake, preheat the oven to 400 degrees. Sprinkle a baking sheet with cornmeal and set aside. Fill a large cast-iron skillet halfway with water and place on the bottom of the oven.

Punch down the dough and divide it in half. With a rolling pin, roll each piece into a rectangular shape about ½ inch thick. Using your hands, roll the rectangles into logs, pinching the ends of the logs to seal. Transfer to the baking sheet and brush lightly with water.

Bake for 30 to 35 minutes, or until the bread makes a hollow sound when tapped, brushing with water several times as the bread bakes. Cool completely on a wire rack before slicing.

Makes 2 loaves

French Bread

THE CLASSIC LONG, slim French loaf has the crust, crumb, and class that few breads can match, and it can be served with all kinds of soups and salads, from the simple to the sublime.

½ teaspoon sugar
1¼ cups lukewarm water
1 package dry yeast
    About 2¾ cups bread flour or
      all-purpose flour
1½ teaspoons kosher salt
    Cornmeal for sprinkling

In a large mixing bowl, stir the sugar into the water. Add the yeast, and stir to dissolve. Let stand until foamy, 3 to 5 minutes. Beat in 1 cup of the flour and the salt. Gradually add the remaining 1¾ cups flour, stirring after each addition. Transfer the dough to a lightly floured surface and knead until smooth and elastic. Use additional flour, if necessary, to prevent the dough from sticking.

Put the dough in a lightly buttered medium bowl. Grease the surface, cover with a damp cloth, and set aside in a warm place to rise for about 1 hour, or until almost doubled.

At least 15 minutes before you bake, preheat the oven to 400 degrees. Sprinkle a baking sheet with the cornmeal and set aside. Fill a large cast-iron skillet halfway with water and place on the bottom of the oven.

Punch down the dough and divide it in half. With a rolling pin, roll each piece into a rectangular shape about ½ inch thick. Using your hands, roll the rectangles into logs, pinching the ends of the logs to seal. Transfer to the baking sheet and brush lightly with water.

Bake for 25 to 30 minutes, or until the bread makes a hollow sound when tapped, brushing with water several times as the bread cooks. Cool completely on a wire rack before slicing.

Makes 2 loaves

Crusty Wheat Wheat Bread

THIS ROUND, brown loaf sprinkled throughout with sunflower seeds is a hearty,
old-fashioned bread that can be served with either sweet or savory spreads.
It's just the kind of bread you want to dip in your soup.

---

2   teaspoons honey

1   cup lukewarm water

1   package dry yeast

    About 1 cup bread flour or
     all-purpose flour

⅓   cup raw sunflower seeds

1   teaspoon kosher salt

1   cup whole wheat flour

    Cornmeal for sprinkling

In a large mixing bowl, stir the honey into the water. Add the yeast and stir to dissolve. Let stand until foamy, 3 to 5 minutes. Beat in the 1 cup white flour. Add the sunflower seeds and salt. Gradually stir in the whole wheat flour. Transfer to a lightly floured surface and knead until the dough is smooth and elastic, using additional white flour, if necessary, to prevent the dough from sticking.

Put the dough in a lightly buttered medium bowl. Grease the surface, cover with a damp cloth, and set aside in a warm place to rise for about 1 hour, or until almost doubled.

At least 15 minutes before you bake, preheat the oven to 400 degrees. Sprinkle a baking sheet with the cornmeal and set aside.

Punch down the dough and shape into a round loaf. Transfer to the baking sheet, brush with water, and bake for 20 minutes. Reduce the heat to 350 degrees, brush with water again, and bake for an additional 15 minutes, or until the bread makes a hollow sound when tapped. Cool thoroughly on a wire rack before slicing.

Makes 1 loaf

Rye Bread

Rye BREAD should be earthy, not earthbound. The goal is to avoid ending up with "lead bread," to make a bread that is chewy and moist instead of dense and wet. A combination of rye flour and bread flour does the trick. It might be difficult to decide whether to serve unsalted butter or Lemon Garlic Neufchâtel Spread (page 251) with this moist, flavorful bread. What a problem to have! Meanwhile, bring out Chilled Beet Soup with Beet Greens (page 96) and Tossed Green Salad with Pine Nut Dressing (page 184). Any way you present it, you'll have a fine meal.

---

2 tablespoons blackstrap molasses

1½ cups lukewarm water or potato water (the liquid reserved from boiling potatoes)

1 package dry yeast

1 tablespoon caraway seeds

1½ teaspoons kosher salt

½ teaspoon fennel seeds

½ teaspoon grated orange rind

1 tablespoon unsalted butter, melted

1¼ cups rye flour

About 2¾ cups bread flour or all-purpose flour

Cornmeal for sprinkling

Milk for brushing loaves

In a large mixing bowl, combine the molasses with the water. Add the yeast and stir to dissolve. Let stand until foamy, 3 to 5 minutes. Add the caraway seeds, salt, fennel seeds, orange rind, and butter. Mix well. Stir in the rye flour. Gradually add 2½ cups of the white flour, stirring after each addition. Transfer the dough to a lightly floured surface and knead in the remaining ¼ cup white flour, or more as needed; the dough will be slightly sticky.

Put the dough in a lightly buttered medium bowl. Grease the surface, cover with a damp cloth, and set aside in a warm place to rise for about 1 hour, or until almost doubled.

At least 15 minutes before you bake, preheat the oven to 375 degrees. Sprinkle a baking sheet with the cornmeal and set aside.

Punch down the dough and form two round loaves 5 inches in diameter. Transfer to the baking sheet and brush with the milk. Bake for 45 minutes, or until the bread makes a hollow sound when tapped. Cool thoroughly on a wire rack before slicing.

Makes 2 loaves

Potato-Onion Rye Bread

ADDING MASHED POTATOES to the dough makes this an earthy, moist loaf. Rye bread can stand some Bruegel-like busyness, and it's the seeds, orange peel, and onions that give these loaves their character. Cut into thick slices and serve with Winter Vegetable Soup (page 77) and Mixed Green Salad (page 180).

---

1 small unpeeled russet potato,
     scrubbed and cut into chunks
2 cups water
1 tablespoon honey
1 package dry yeast
1 tablespoon unsalted butter
1 cup chopped yellow onion
1 tablespoon caraway seeds
1½ teaspoons kosher salt,
     plus more for sprinkling
1½ cups rye flour
   About 3¼ cups bread flour or
     all-purpose flour
   Cornmeal for sprinkling
   Milk for brushing

Boil the potato in the water for 5 to 7 minutes, or until tender. Drain, reserving 1½ cups of the potato water. Cool slightly to lukewarm. Meanwhile, mash the potato and set aside ½ cup. (Discard the rest, if there is any.)

In a large mixing bowl, combine the lukewarm potato water with the honey. Add the yeast and stir to dissolve. Let stand until foamy, 3 to 5 minutes.

Meanwhile, in a small skillet, melt the butter. Add the onion and caraway seeds. Cook over low heat until the onion starts to soften, 3 to 4 minutes. Sprinkle with the 1½ teaspoons salt. Cool, then stir the onion mixture and reserved mashed potato into the yeast mixture. Gradually stir in the

rye flour and 2¼ cups of the white flour. Transfer the dough to a lightly floured surface and knead in the remaining 1 cup white flour. The dough will be slightly sticky.

Put the dough in a lightly buttered medium bowl. Grease the surface, cover with a damp cloth, and set aside in a warm place to rise for about 1 hour, or until almost doubled.

At least 15 minutes before you bake, preheat the oven to 375 degrees. Sprinkle a baking sheet with the cornmeal and set aside.

Punch down the dough and shape into 2 long loaves, adding more bread flour as needed. Transfer to the baking sheet, cover with a damp cloth, and let rise for 20 minutes. Brush the loaves with the milk and sprinkle with kosher salt.

Bake for 45 minutes, or until the bread makes a hollow sound when tapped. Cool thoroughly on a wire rack before slicing.

Makes 2 loaves

A S IN LIFE, SO IT IS IN COOKING: There is no substitute for experience. I have always regarded that truism as a license to have fun with food. Play is, after all, a very serious business. I once did an experiment with a friend of mine that involved taking equal amounts of pastry flour, all-purpose flour, and bread flour and mixing them with equal amounts of water to test their relative viscosity. We plunged a spoon in the midst of each clump of flour "paste" and stood back to watch the results. You might think this was some kind of childhood dalliance, but we adults were trying to get a grip on the absorbent properties of various kinds of flour, and being tactile and literal folks, just had to see it to believe it. We observed that the more refined the flour, the less stable a base it provided for the spoon. In the end, superior gluten won, and the spoon in the bread flour listed last. It was a moment of truth that breathed life into those tidy little biological diagrams of wheat grains and the gluten-related passages I'd read in some of my cookbooks. At last, experimental evidence to support the theoretical side of the story and a thoroughly satisfying explanation for what I felt beneath my hands when I kneaded bread or mixed batter.

Spiral Herb Bread

THIS CLASSIC homemade white bread, archetypal silhouette and all, is flavored with herbs. It's particularly good with Autumn Vegetable Minestra (page 73).

---

1 teaspoon honey

1 cup lukewarm water

1 package dry yeast

1 large egg

1 teaspoon kosher salt

About 3 cups bread flour or all-purpose flour

1 tablespoon butter, at room temperature

½ teaspoon dried basil

½ teaspoon dried oregano

½ teaspoon dried thyme

½ teaspoon dried chives

In a large mixing bowl, combine the honey with the water. Add the yeast, stirring to dissolve. Let stand until foamy, 3 to 5 minutes. In a small bowl, beat the egg with the salt and add to the yeast mixture. Beat in 1 cup of the flour and gradually add the remaining 2 cups flour, stirring after each addition. Transfer the dough to a lightly floured surface and knead in the butter. Continue to knead until the dough is smooth and elastic.

Put the dough in a lightly buttered large bowl. Grease the surface, cover with a damp cloth, and set aside in a warm place to rise for about 1 hour, or until almost doubled.

At least 15 minutes before you bake, preheat the oven to 350 degrees. Butter a 5-x-9-inch loaf pan and set aside.

Punch down the dough and flatten it into a rectangle about 1 inch thick. Sprinkle the herbs over the surface and roll the dough into a log. Pinch the ends to seal, tuck them under to shape into a loaf, and transfer to the pan.

Bake for 45 minutes, or until the bread makes a hollow sound when tapped. Cool thoroughly on a wire rack before slicing.

Makes 1 loaf

Cardamom Raisin Bread

A SLICE OF Cardamom Raisin Bread spread with Hazelnut Butter (page 260) is a lovely snack to linger over, abundant with the flavors of spices, fruit, and nuts.

---

1   cup orange juice
¾   cup raisins
¼   cup coarsely chopped walnuts
¾   teaspoon ground cardamom
1   package dry yeast
¼   cup lukewarm water
    About 3¼ cups bread flour or
    all-purpose flour
1   teaspoon kosher salt
    Cornmeal for sprinkling

Mix the juice, raisins, nuts, and cardamom together in a small saucepan. Bring to a boil. Remove from the heat, cover, and set aside for 20 minutes, or until the juice is absorbed.

In a large mixing bowl, dissolve the yeast in the water. Let stand until foamy, 3 to 5 minutes. Stir in 1 cup of the flour. Add the salt and mix in the raisins and nuts and any remaining liquid.

Gradually add 1½ cups of the flour, ½ cup at a time, stirring after each addition. Transfer the dough to a lightly floured surface and knead in the remaining ¾ cup flour, or more as needed, until the dough is smooth and elastic.

Put the dough in a lightly buttered medium bowl. Grease the surface, cover with a damp cloth, and set aside to rise for about 1 hour, or until almost doubled.

At least 15 minutes before you bake, preheat the oven to 375 degrees. Sprinkle a baking sheet with the cornmeal and set aside.

Punch down the dough, shape it into a round loaf, and transfer it to the baking sheet. Bake for 35 to 40 minutes, or until the bread makes a hollow sound when tapped. Cool thoroughly on a wire rack before slicing.

Makes 1 loaf

Anadama Bread with Orange Zest

I HAVE A VINTAGE COOKBOOK, first published in 1939, which proclaims itself to be "a greater American cookbook, consisting of ten principal sections, each devoted to a characteristic American style of cooking." American culinary zones have shifted somewhat since the author Ruth Berzolheimer's day, and regional cooking doesn't look the way it used to. According to Ms. Berzolheimer, Anadama bread hails from New England. My version of this American standard with its blue cornmeal and orange peel would probably confound her with its boundary-crossing properties, but that's progress!

½ cup blue or yellow cornmeal

2 cups cold water, plus ¼ cup
　 lukewarm water

2 tablespoons butter

½ cup molasses

2 tablespoons grated orange rind

1 package dry yeast

1 teaspoon kosher salt
　 About 4¼ cups bread flour or
　 all-purpose flour

Whisk together the cornmeal and the 2 cups cold water in the top of a double boiler. Cook over medium heat for 10 minutes. Stir in the butter, molasses, and orange rind. Cook for an additional 20 minutes, or until the mixture thickens. Transfer to a large mixing bowl. Stir to release the steam and cool to lukewarm.

In a small bowl, dissolve the yeast in the ¼ cup lukewarm water. Let stand until foamy, 3 to 4 minutes. Add to the cornmeal and mix thoroughly. Stir in the salt. Gradually add the 4¼ cups of flour, stirring after each addition. Transfer the dough to a lightly floured surface and knead until smooth and elastic. Use more flour (about 2 tablespoons), if necessary, to prevent the dough from sticking.

Put the dough in a lightly buttered medium bowl. Grease the surface, cover with a damp cloth, and set aside in a warm place to rise for about 1 hour, or until almost doubled.

At least 15 minutes before you bake, preheat the oven to 350 degrees. Lightly oil two 8½-x-4½-inch loaf pans with vegetable spray and set aside.

Punch down the dough and form 2 loaves. Transfer to the baking pans and bake for about 40 minutes, or until the bread makes a hollow sound when tapped. Cool thoroughly on a wire rack before slicing.

Makes 2 loaves

Pumpkin Bread

THIS RECIPE demonstrates that a few substitutions and additions can alter a basic bread recipe with intriguing results. The secret is maintaining the balance between the wet and dry ingredients and kneading the dough until it is smooth and elastic, which keeps you in touch with how well things are blending together.

---

1 cup apple cider
1 tablespoon maple syrup
1 package dry yeast
   About 3¼ cups bread flour or
      all-purpose flour
½ cup quick-cooking rolled oats
⅓ cup canned pumpkin or cooked
      and pureed fresh pumpkin
1 tablespoon butter, melted
¼ cup pumpkin seeds
¼ cup raw sunflower seeds
1½ teaspoons kosher salt
   Cornmeal for sprinkling
   Milk for
      brushing

In a small saucepan, heat the cider until it simmers. Pour into a large mixing bowl and stir in the maple syrup. Cool to lukewarm, add the yeast, and stir to dissolve. Let stand until foamy, 3 to 4 minutes. Beat in 1 cup of the flour. Stir in the oats, pumpkin, butter, pumpkin seeds, sunflower seeds, and salt. Blend well.

Gradually add 2 cups of the remaining flour, stirring after each addition. Turn the dough onto a lightly floured surface and knead in the remaining ¼ cup flour, or more as needed, until the dough is smooth and elastic.

Ladle, Leaf, & Loaf

Put the dough in a lightly buttered medium bowl. Grease the surface, cover with a damp cloth, and set aside to rise in a warm place for about 1 hour, or until almost doubled.

At least 15 minutes before you bake, preheat the oven to 350 degrees. Sprinkle a baking sheet with the cornmeal and set aside.

Punch down the dough and shape into a round loaf. Transfer the loaf to the baking sheet, brush the top with the milk, and bake for about 1 hour, or until the bread makes a hollow sound when tapped. Cool thoroughly on a wire rack before slicing.

Makes 1 loaf

Onion Flatbread

SERVING A STORE-BOUGHT bread is no match for the small triumph one feels upon serving a "gourmet-style" homemade bread like this one, accompanied by an elegant spread.

---

1 package dry yeast

1 cup lukewarm water

1 tablespoon plus 2 teaspoons olive oil

½ teaspoon dried basil

½ teaspoon dried oregano

1½ teaspoons kosher salt

About 2¾ cups bread flour or all-purpose flour

1 medium yellow onion, thinly sliced

1 large garlic clove, sliced

½ tablespoon finely minced fresh rosemary

Cornmeal for sprinkling

In a large bowl, dissolve the yeast in the water. Stir and let stand until foamy, 3 to 5 minutes. Add 2 teaspoons of the oil, the basil, oregano, and ½ teaspoon of the salt. Gradually add the 2¾ cups flour, stirring after each addition. Transfer the dough to a lightly floured surface and knead, adding more flour as needed, until smooth and elastic.

Put the dough in a lightly buttered medium bowl. Grease the surface, cover with a damp cloth, and set aside in a warm place to rise for about 1 hour, or until almost doubled.

At least 15 minutes before you bake, preheat the oven to 400 degrees. Sprinkle a baking sheet with the cornmeal and set aside.

In a small skillet, heat the remaining 1 tablespoon oil. Add the onion, garlic, and rosemary. Cook until the onion softens and the mixture is aromatic, 3 to 5 minutes. Remove from the heat and set aside.

Punch down the dough and divide it in half. Roll out each piece into an 8-to-9-inch circle. Transfer the circles to the baking sheet, 3 inches apart.

Spread half of the onion mixture on each bread and sprinkle with the remaining 1 teaspoon salt. Bake for 20 minutes, or until lightly browned. Serve warm.

Makes 2 flatbreads

Black Bread with Raisins

I HAD MY DEFINING raisin bread moment when I discovered raisin pumpernickel in a Jewish deli in Los Angeles. No squishy white bread with a smattering of raisins, this dark, dense loaf, with just enough dough to stick the raisins together, is a near-confection.

---

1 cup water

½ cup strong coffee

2 tablespoons blackstrap molasses

1 package dry yeast

1¼ cups raisins

2 tablespoons cocoa powder

2 tablespoons cider vinegar

½ tablespoon grated orange rind

1½ teaspoons kosher salt

1 teaspoon anise seeds

2 cups rye flour

About 2¼ cups bread flour
or all-purpose flour

Cornmeal for sprinkling

In a small saucepan, heat the water, coffee, and molasses until it simmers. Transfer to a large mixing bowl. When the mixture is lukewarm, add the yeast and stir to dissolve. Let stand until foamy, 3 to 5 minutes. Mix in the raisins, cocoa powder, vinegar, orange rind, salt, and anise seeds. Stir in the rye flour and gradually add 2 cups of the white flour. Transfer the dough to a lightly floured surface and knead, using the remaining ¼ cup white flour, or more as needed, until smooth and elastic.

Put the dough in a lightly buttered medium bowl. Grease the surface, cover with a damp cloth, and set aside in a warm place to rise for about 1 hour, or until almost doubled.

At least 15 minutes before you bake, preheat the oven to 375 degrees. Sprinkle a baking sheet with the cornmeal and set aside.

Punch down the dough and form 2 round loaves about 5 inches in diameter. Transfer to the baking sheet and bake for about 40 minutes, or until the bread makes a hollow sound when tapped. Cool thoroughly on a wire rack before slicing.

Makes 2 loaves

Olive Bread

THERE IS NOTHING more disappointing than olive breads that don't live up to their name simply because they lose their olives. It's frustrating to be arrested in midbite and have the choice part of the loaf never make it to your mouth. No more escaping olives and the empty little caves they leave behind! The sautéed onions and minced olives in this recipe give the bread a moist and chewy texture, and that's what keeps those whole olives right where they belong.

---

1 tablespoon olive oil

1 small yellow onion, chopped

2 garlic cloves, pressed

½ teaspoon minced fresh rosemary

1 teaspoon honey

1¼ cups lukewarm water

1 package dry yeast

About 3¼ cups bread flour or all-purpose flour

½ cup whole pitted kalamata olives

1 teaspoon kosher salt

Cornmeal for sprinkling

In a small skillet, heat the oil. Cook the onion, garlic, and rosemary until the onion softens and the mixture is aromatic, 3 to 5 minutes. Remove from the heat and set aside.

In a large mixing bowl, stir the honey into the water. Add the yeast and stir to dissolve. Let stand until foamy, 3 to 5 minutes. Beat in 1 cup of the flour. Mince enough olives to equal ¼ cup and stir the onion mixture, remaining olives, and salt into the flour mixture. Mix well and beat in 1 more cup flour. Gradually add the remaining 1¼ cups flour, ¼ cup at a time, stirring after each addition.

Transfer the dough to a lightly floured surface

and knead until smooth and elastic, using additional flour, if necessary, to prevent the dough from sticking.

Put the dough in a lightly buttered medium bowl. Grease the surface, cover with a damp cloth, and set aside in a warm place to rise for about 1 hour, or until almost doubled.

At least 15 minutes before you bake, preheat the oven to 400 degrees. Place a large cast-iron skillet half filled with water on the bottom of the oven. Sprinkle a baking sheet with the cornmeal and set aside.

Punch down the dough and form two loaves, 10 inches in diameter. Transfer the loaves to the baking sheet; with a sharp knife slash the tops and brush with water. Bake for 45 minutes, or until the bread makes a hollow sound when tapped, brushing with water once or twice during baking. Cool thoroughly on a wire rack before slicing.

Makes 2 loaves

Quick Breads

I THINK THE ORIGINAL QUICK BREAD must have been matzo, if you include crackers in this generous family. Things have gotten a bit more elaborate since the old days, but even with the addition of milk, eggs, oil, fruits, and vegetables, the bottom line remains the same: no waiting for the dough to rise. Baking powder and baking soda circumvent that step, so with quick breads, it's batter up and go! The whole business is streamlined—no long-term commitment to kneading necessary here, no tapping and thumping the crust to listen for that hollow sound that says the bread is done, and no waiting patiently until the loaf is cool before slicing. Quick breads are ready to take out of the oven when a toothpick inserted in the center of the loaf comes out clean. They can be served piping hot—and they make great partners with all kinds of spreads. There are even a few that flirt with dessert, like Lemon Quick Bread, toeing the line between the savory and the sweet.

Spoonbread

Oh, THE DELIGHTS of egg whites and their powers of persuasion! In this recipe, they make light of cornmeal and deliciously obscure the line between bread and soufflé. This bread is best when served hot from the oven.

1½ cups water
1 cup yellow cornmeal
1 teaspoon sugar
1 teaspoon kosher salt
½ cup skim milk
2 tablespoons canola oil
1 tablespoon butter, melted
2 large eggs, separated

Preheat the oven to 350 degrees. Lightly oil a 9-inch-square baking pan with vegetable spray, and set aside.

In a medium saucepan, boil the water. Stir in the cornmeal, sugar, and salt. Remove from the heat as soon as the mixture thickens. Stir in the milk, oil, and melted butter.

Beat the egg yolks in a small bowl until lemon colored. Stirring rapidly, add them to the cornmeal mixture. Beat the egg whites in a medium bowl until they form soft peaks, and fold them into the batter. Spoon the batter into the pan and bake for 40 to 45 minutes, or until the top is browned and a toothpick inserted in the center of the bread comes out clean. Serve immediately.

Serves 4–6

Green Chili Corn Bread

THIS SAVORY corn bread manages not to be dense and heavy even though it's loaded with goodies. Serve with Herbed Butternut Squash Soup (page 56) for a great cold weather meal.

1 cup yellow cornmeal

1 cup all-purpose flour

2 teaspoons baking powder

½ teaspoon ground cumin

½ teaspoon kosher salt

¼ teaspoon dried oregano

1 cup skim milk

1 large egg

½ cup grated sharp cheddar cheese

½ cup diced, drained canned green chilies

½ cup fresh or canned corn kernels

¼ cup canola oil

Preheat the oven to 400 degrees. Lightly oil an 8-inch-square baking pan with vegetable spray and set aside.

Combine the dry ingredients in a large bowl. In a separate bowl, mix together the remaining ingredients. Gradually stir this mixture into the dry ingredients and mix well. Spoon the batter into the baking pan and bake for 20 to 25 minutes, or until a toothpick inserted in the center of the bread comes out clean. Serve hot from the oven.

Serves 6

Ladle, Leaf, & Loaf

Corn Sticks

THE PAN'S the thing that gives these individual corn breads their delicate crumb, crust, and charm.

1 cup skim milk

1 large egg

1½ tablespoons honey

1 teaspoon canola oil

½ cup all-purpose flour

1½ cups yellow or blue cornmeal

2 teaspoons baking powder

½ teaspoon kosher salt

Preheat the oven to 450 degrees. Lightly oil a cast-iron corn stick pan with vegetable spray or brush with melted butter and set aside. You can use two pans or make two batches of corn sticks, one at a time.

In a medium bowl, mix together the milk, egg, honey, and oil. In a separate medium bowl, combine the flour, cornmeal, baking powder, and salt. Stir the liquid ingredients into the dry ingredients and blend well.

Spoon the batter into the pan, filling each section three-fourths full. Bake for 12 minutes, or until lightly browned. Remove from the pan and cool briefly on a wire rack before serving.

Makes 14 corn sticks

Ladle, Leaf, & Loaf

FORM AND FUNCTION

SOME RECIPES REACH BACK in a straight line to another era and yet manage not to seem dated. Popovers and corn sticks have been around for quite a while, and I've never seen them raise any quizzical eyebrows at the table; everyone is far more interested in passing the butter and getting on with it. I've made these recipes with my own adjustments and variations, but regardless of what culinary changes I've wrought, the shape of these breads remains the same. Cast-iron pans can't be improved on when it comes to baking these little breads, but the design of traditional pans has always puzzled me.

Why is it that a popover pan has eleven sections and a corn stick pan has seven? They break the rule of an even dozen or half dozen by just enough to throw things off. The owner of the local kitchen store told me he thought that popover pans have their peculiar configuration because that arrangement was the most efficient way to use the materials "in the old days," meaning colonial times. So some ingenious fellow solved a tricky casting problem way back when, and the eleven-cup popover pan has been the standard ever since.

There were no historic tidbits my source could recall for the corn stick pan, although I did learn they come in increments of five, seven, nine, and even eleven sections. We speculated a bit about this and decided that perhaps some resourceful person working during the heyday of cast-iron cookery made a pan that would accommodate his own family's needs, and it worked so well, no one's ever bothered to change it.

I guess these pans are successful examples from the if-it's-not-broken-don't-fix-it department, a small holdout in our world of relentless modification and planned obsolescence.

Cornmeal Popovers

CORNMEAL ADDS a slight crunch and sweet flavor to this variation of the classic popover—the perfect bread to serve with light soups and salads. Try them with Red and Yellow Tomato Soup with Broiled Tomatoes (page 50) and Goat Cheese Salad (page 160) for a summer meal.

¾ **cup all-purpose flour**

¼ **cup yellow cornmeal**

¼ **teaspoon kosher salt**

2 **large eggs**

1 **cup skim milk**

1 **tablespoon canola oil**

Preheat the oven to 450 degrees. Lightly butter a muffin or popover pan.

In a medium bowl, combine the flour, cornmeal, and salt. In a separate bowl, beat the eggs with the milk and oil, using an electric mixer. Heat the muffin pan in the oven for several minutes. Meanwhile, add the liquid ingredients to the dry ingredients and beat with the mixer until smooth.

Remove the muffin pan from the oven. Fill 11 of the muffin cups with the batter. (Traditional cast-iron popover pans are made with 11 cups.) Bake for 20 minutes. Remove the popovers from the pan, place them in a basket lined with a clean napkin, and serve immediately.

Makes 4 popovers

Blue Corn Bread

BLUE CORNMEAL has a very subtle flavor and fine texture, but I like it more for nostalgic reasons; it reminds me of New Mexico. For years after I left New Mexico, I harbored an insatiable longing for the place. It was so deep, I was inspired to grow a small plot of blue corn in upstate New York one summer from seeds my brother sent me from Albuquerque. I even dried the corn, ground it into meal, and made corn bread. It's amazing the lengths to which one will go to nurture memories and how often that path leads us to the foods we eat.

---

1 cup all-purpose flour
1 cup blue cornmeal
3 teaspoons baking powder
1 teaspoon kosher salt
¾ teaspoon dried rubbed sage
½ teaspoon chili powder
¼ cup pine nuts
1 cup skim milk
1 large egg
2 tablespoons canola oil
1½ tablespoons honey

Preheat the oven to 400 degrees. Lightly oil a 10-inch pie plate with vegetable spray and set aside.

In a large bowl, combine the dry ingredients, including the pine nuts. In a separate bowl, beat together the milk, egg, oil, and honey. Stir the liquid ingredients into the dry ingredients to make a smooth batter. Pour the batter into the pie plate. Bake for about 25 minutes, or until the top of the bread is lightly browned. Cool briefly before serving.

Serves 6

❧ CORN ❧

I LIKE WALKING UP AND DOWN my country road during the year, watching the seasons mirrored in the progress of the corn crops growing in the fields. The corn is supposed to be "knee-high by the fourth of July," and it usually makes it. In late summer, the plants are so tall, they obscure the horizon and become an aviary filled with darting, chattering birds. The stalks rattle

in the wind by October, and after the harvest, the wild turkeys show up to glean the fields.

Someone asked me one summer how many ears of corn grow on a stalk, and I actually had to take a walk down the road to look. I pictured several ears growing opposite one another up the stalk toward the tassel, but that fanciful notion is quite incorrect. There is only one ear on each stalk. My entire perception shifted toward the Lilliputian; corn is a grass, with each plant bearing one seed head. A cornfield, in another dimension, could be a lawn.

That one ear per stalk is something I always look forward to each summer as freshly cooked corn on the cob, but there is so much more! Fresh corn kernels in salads, corn soups and chowders, soup made with hominy, corn breads—it's quite a crew, and there's a dish among them for every time of year.

Peanut Butter Corn Bread

THIS RECIPE comes directly from my vegetarian restaurant days, when someone
in the kitchen proposed mixing the peanut butter into the corn bread instead of using it as
a spread. It's a great combination, and simultaneously "retro" and "au courant"
served with Tahini Honey Spread (page 259).

1¼ cups all-purpose flour

¾ cup yellow cornmeal

3 teaspoons baking powder

¾ teaspoon kosher salt

⅓ cup coarsely chopped salted peanuts

1 cup minus 2 tablespoons skim
  buttermilk

3 tablespoons honey

2 tablespoons unsalted,
  unsweetened peanut butter

1 large egg

Preheat the oven to 375 degrees. Lightly oil a 10-inch pie plate with vegetable spray and set aside.

In a large bowl, combine the flour, cornmeal, baking powder, salt, and chopped peanuts. In a separate bowl, beat together the remaining ingredients. Stir the liquid ingredients into the dry ingredients and mix well. Spoon the batter into the pie plate and bake for 20 minutes, or until a toothpick inserted in the center of the bread comes out clean. Cool slightly before slicing.

Serves 6

Seeded Soda Bread

SODA BREADS are perfect partners for fall and winter soups. They are substantial without being heavy, and they keep well, often tasting better a day or two after they've been baked. They also make surprisingly good toast and lend themselves nicely to nontraditional interpretations. The mixture of seeds and black pepper that infuses this bread gives each bite some zing.

---

2 cups all-purpose flour

1½ teaspoons baking powder

½ teaspoon baking soda

¾ teaspoon kosher salt

¼ teaspoon freshly ground black pepper

3 tablespoons hulled sesame seeds

2 teaspoons caraway seeds

¾ teaspoon celery seeds

¼ cup canola oil

1 large egg

½ cup nonfat buttermilk, plus extra for brushing

Preheat the oven to 375 degrees. Lightly oil a 10-inch pie plate with vegetable spray and set aside.

In a large bowl, combine the flour, baking powder, baking soda, salt, pepper, and seeds. Drizzle the oil over the mixture and blend it into the flour with your fingers.

In a separate bowl, beat the egg into the buttermilk. Pour the liquid ingredients into the dry ingredients and mix to form a stiff dough. Knead briefly. Shape into a round loaf 8 inches in diameter. Score with a knife, dividing the dough into quarters, and brush with the extra buttermilk.

Place in the pie plate and bake for 30 to 35 minutes, or until a toothpick inserted in the center of the bread comes out clean. Cool on a wire rack before serving.

Makes 1 loaf

Spicy Soda Bread

I WAS DELIGHTED to discover that my favorite peppercorn could be used so successfully as a flavoring agent for soda bread.

---

2 cups all-purpose flour

1½ teaspoons baking powder

½ teaspoon baking soda

½ teaspoon kosher salt

2 teaspoons crushed pink or
   black peppercorns

½ tablespoon ground coriander

¼ cup canola oil

½ cup nonfat buttermilk,
   plus extra for brushing

1 large egg

1 tablespoon honey

Preheat the oven to 375 degrees. Lightly oil a 10-inch pie plate with vegetable spray and set aside.

In a large bowl, combine the flour, baking powder, baking soda, salt, peppercorns, and coriander. Drizzle the oil over the mixture and blend it into the flour with your fingers.

Pour the buttermilk into a separate bowl and beat in the egg and honey. Pour the liquid ingredients into the dry ingredients and mix to form a stiff dough. Knead briefly. Shape into a round loaf 8 inches in diameter. Score the surface, dividing it into quarters, and brush with the extra buttermilk.

Place in the pie plate and bake for 30 to 35 minutes, or until a toothpick inserted in the center of the bread comes out clean. Cool on a wire rack before serving.

Makes 1 loaf

Whole Wheat Soda Bread

The beauty of soda bread is that the basic recipe is so well suited to adaptations;
it doesn't take much to make an ordinary loaf of Whole Wheat Soda Bread
into something special. Serve with Hazelnut Butter (page 260).

---

1 cup whole wheat flour

1 cup all-purpose flour

½ cup coarsely ground walnuts

1½ teaspoons baking powder

½ teaspoon baking soda

1 teaspoon five-spice powder
   (available in Asian grocery stores)

¾ teaspoon kosher salt

3 tablespoons canola oil

6 tablespoons dried currants

1 tablespoon maple syrup

⅔ cup nonfat buttermilk,
   plus extra for brushing

1 large egg

Preheat the oven to 375 degrees. Lightly oil a 10-inch pie plate with vegetable spray and set aside.

In a large bowl, combine the flours, walnuts, baking powder, baking soda, five-spice powder, and salt. Drizzle the oil over the mixture and blend it into the flour with your fingers. Stir in the currants.

In a separate bowl, beat together the maple syrup, buttermilk, and egg. Pour the liquid ingredients into the dry ingredients, and mix to form a stiff dough. Knead briefly. Shape into a round loaf 8 inches in diameter. Score the surface, dividing the dough into quarters, and brush with the extra buttermilk. Place in the pie plate and bake for 30 to 35 minutes, or until a toothpick inserted in the center of the bread comes out clean. Cool on a wire rack before serving.

Makes 1 loaf

❧ ART SAVES LIVES ❧

*I*BOUGHT A DUSTPAN THE OTHER DAY that I didn't need. It was in the grocery store, and I feel as though I rescued it from a humble life and elevated it to an art object. Whether I make art or collect it, I firmly subscribe to the idea that "Art Saves Lives." These words of wisdom are inscribed on a pin I received as a gift from a friend—and I have been "saved" by beauty in art as often as I have by humor.

My dustpan has a painting on it of a cluster of piglets tearing across a lawn toward their beaming mother. There's a Grandma Moses–style house in the background, some puffy white clouds in the sky, and a checkered border framing the scene. On the back of the dustpan it says, "J. V. Reed. Collecting Dust Since 1875, Louisville, KY, U.S.A."

I keep lots of other objects in my kitchen, along with this new acquisition, for amusement and a daily dose of aesthetics. On one wall is a series of four hand-painted Italian plates of a pear in a continually evolving state of "devourment," down to a mere handful of seeds. Above the counter I have a painting of empty eggshells from my friend Ruthie's minimalist period. Some of my own work is in the kitchen, too, next to a postcard of a Matisse paper cut. I like to keep good company.

I extend this appreciation for aesthetics to my cooking utensils and dishes, which, in order to make the grade, have to move seamlessly between being functional and being attractive. Occasionally it's a trade-off, but by now, most of what's in the kitchen has survived a regimen of upgrades and replacements, so I have good tools to work with.

The same standard applies to my studio, where the quality of my scissors is of great concern. I go through scissors like the storybook twelve dancing princesses who wore out their dancing shoes every night. It ruins scissors to have them sharpened because that changes the bevel and thickness of the

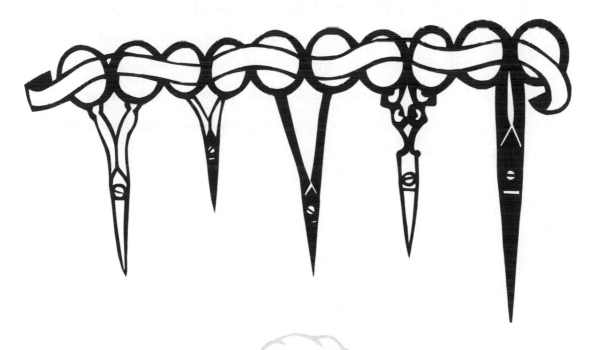

blades, so I hang up the old ones on the bulletin board when they become dull and order new ones. I have quite a display of retired scissors now, some of which I used so often, I wore the gold off the handles. Before I settled on a particular style and brand, I experimented with many different kinds, and those are also up on the bulletin board, along with some eccentric ones I've collected and received as gifts.

Oddly enough, I don't have a pair of decent kitchen scissors—a situation I, of all people, could remedy. I have scissors for cutting wire, scissors for cutting glass, wicked-looking paper-cutting scissors with blades eight inches long, and a pair of gargantuan upholstery shears that must weigh more than a pound—but not a kitchen scissors among them. Perhaps I've deliberately not come full circle from the studio to the kitchen with tools because I prefer to use scissors in my studio rather than knives and knives in the kitchen instead of scissors. As I cut, I hold the paper up and turn it all around; I can't imagine how I'd achieve that kind of freedom with a knife. I've never been in a circus, so unless there is some way to make food levitate while I whack at it, there's no hope for me above and beyond the cutting board.

Savory Zucchini Bread

ZUCCHINI BREADS that are made with coarsely grated zucchini seem to have an air of desperation about them, as though some sort of hasty shredding spree has taken place in a government office. They make bread that's too wet and too bland. The fine blade of a food processor or hand-held grater transforms the bread from a place to stash excess vegetables to a delectable companion for tomato and bean soups.

Grated Parmesan cheese for sprinkling
1 **tablespoon olive oil**
1 **medium yellow onion, quartered and sliced**
1 **tablespoon chopped fresh parsley**
1 **tablespoon minced fresh chives**
2 **large fresh basil leaves, minced**
½ **teaspoon minced fresh oregano or ¼ teaspoon dried**
1 **cup finely grated zucchini**
1 **large egg, beaten**
½ **cup grated sharp cheddar cheese**
2 **teaspoons baking powder**
½ **teaspoon kosher salt**
1½ **cups all-purpose flour**

Preheat the oven to 350 degrees. Lightly oil an 8½-x-4½-inch loaf pan with vegetable spray, dust with the grated Parmesan, and set aside.

Heat the oil in a small skillet. Cook the onion with the herbs over medium heat until the onion starts to soften, 3 to 4 minutes. Remove from the heat and set aside.

Drain the grated zucchini in a sieve over a small bowl. Press gently with a spoon to force out the excess liquid. In a large bowl, combine the onion mixture with the zucchini. Mix in the egg and grated cheddar. Add the baking powder and salt. Gradually add the flour, ½ cup at a time, stirring after each addition; the batter will be stiff.

Spoon the batter into the pan, pressing it gently into the corners. Bake for 40 minutes, or until a toothpick inserted in the center of the bread comes out clean. Cool on a wire rack before serving.

Makes 1 loaf

Zucchini Quick Bread

THIS RECIPE uses one of my favorite "secret" quick bread ingredients: ground nuts. Substituting nuts for a portion of the flour gives the bread a lighter texture and more delicate crumb because of the added fat, but don't panic! Nuts have monounsaturated fat, which is among the beneficial fats in food.

1½   cups finely grated fresh zucchini

1   large egg, beaten

2   tablespoons canola oil

¾   cup finely chopped walnuts

3   tablespoons dark brown sugar

2   teaspoons baking powder

½   teaspoon baking soda

     Scant ¼ teaspoon kosher salt

½   teaspoon ground cinnamon

½   teaspoon pure vanilla extract

1½   cups all-purpose flour

Preheat the oven to 350 degrees. Lightly oil an 8½-x-4½-inch loaf pan with vegetable spray and set aside.

Drain the grated zucchini in a sieve over a small bowl. Press gently with a spoon to force out the excess liquid. In a medium bowl, combine the zucchini with the egg and oil. Stir in the walnuts, brown sugar, baking powder, baking soda, and salt. Add the cinnamon and vanilla. Gradually add the flour, ½ cup at a time, stirring after each addition; the batter will be stiff.

Spoon the batter into the pan, pressing it gently into the corners. Bake for 40 minutes, or until a toothpick inserted in the center of the bread comes out clean. Cool on a wire rack before serving.

Makes 1 loaf

Pumpkin Quick Bread

A LITTLE SWEET, a little spicy, Pumpkin Quick Bread provides a nice contrast to dramatic dishes like Roasted Red Pepper Soup with Crisp Julienned Potatoes (page 53) or it can cozy up to Curried Tomato Soup with Toasted Pumpkin Seeds (page 55) because their seasonings are so compatible.

---

1 cup canned pumpkin or cooked
  and pureed fresh pumpkin

1 large egg, beaten

2 tablespoons canola oil

2 teaspoons baking powder

¼ teaspoon baking soda

¼ teaspoon kosher salt

½ cup finely ground pecans

¼ cup dark brown sugar

1 teaspoon ground cinnamon

¾ teaspoon ground ginger

⅛ teaspoon ground cloves

1½ cups all purpose flour

Preheat the oven to 350 degrees. Lightly oil an 8½-x-4½-inch loaf pan with vegetable spray and set aside.

In a large bowl, combine the pumpkin, egg, and oil. Mix well. Stir in the baking powder, baking soda, and salt. Add the pecans, brown sugar, and spices. Gradually stir in the flour. Spoon the batter into the pan and bake for about 30 to 35 minutes, or until a toothpick inserted in the center of the bread comes out clean. Cool on a wire rack before serving.

Makes 1 loaf

Lemon Quick Bread

SERVE THIS BREAD with Saffron Salmon Chowder with Sweet Peppers (page 110),
Asparagus Essence with Toasted Almonds (page 37), or Golden Lemon Chicken Soup (page 102);
its sweet lemony flavor and buttermilk lightness will add a little grace note to the meal.
The bread tastes better the day after baking.

Powdered sugar for sprinkling
1 teaspoon grated lemon rind
2 cups all-purpose flour
¾ cup finely ground pecans
¼ cup sugar
2 teaspoons baking powder
½ teaspoon kosher salt
1 cup minus 2 tablespoons
   nonfat buttermilk
¼ cup plus 2 tablespoons freshly
   squeezed and strained lemon juice
1 large egg
2 tablespoons canola oil

Preheat the oven to 350 degrees. Lightly oil an 8½-x-4½-inch loaf pan with vegetable spray, dust with the powdered sugar, and set aside.

In a large bowl, toss the lemon rind with the flour. Stir in the pecans, sugar, baking powder, and salt.

In a separate bowl, beat together the buttermilk, lemon juice, egg, and oil. Pour the liquid ingredients into the dry ingredients and blend well. Spoon the batter into the pan and bake for about 45 minutes, or until a toothpick inserted in the center of the bread comes out clean. Cool on a wire rack before serving.

Makes 1 loaf

Orange Raisin Quick Bread

THE QUINTESSENTIAL QUICK BREAD: fruit, nuts, spices, some buttermilk, and a little of this and that to hold it all together, and you've got a warm, fragrant loaf to serve with a green salad and vegetable soup.

1½ cups all-purpose flour

¾ cup coarsely chopped walnuts

1 teaspoon grated orange rind

1 teaspoon baking powder

½ teaspoon kosher salt

⅛ teaspoon ground cloves

2 tablespoons canola oil

½ cup raisins

½ cup nonfat buttermilk

¼ cup plus 2 tablespoons freshly squeezed and strained orange juice

1 large egg

1 tablespoon honey

Preheat the oven to 350 degrees. Lightly oil an 8½-x-4½-inch loaf pan with vegetable spray, and set aside.

In a large bowl, combine the flour with the walnuts, orange rind, baking powder, salt, and cloves. Drizzle the oil over the mixture and blend it into the flour with your fingers. Stir in the raisins.

In a separate bowl, mix together the buttermilk, orange juice, egg, and honey. Pour the liquid ingredients into the dry ingredients, and mix well; the batter will be stiff. Spoon the batter into the pan, pressing it gently into the corners. Bake for 35 minutes, or until a toothpick inserted in the center of the bread comes out clean. Cool on a wire rack before serving.

Makes 1 loaf

Sesame Flatbread

Mɑᴅᴇ ᴛᴏ ʙᴇ sᴇʀᴠᴇᴅ with substantial soups like Portobello Mushroom and Barley Soup with Garlic Croutons (page 78), Carrot and Cannellini Bean Soup with Cumin (page 86), and Curried Lentil Soup (page 81), Sesame Flatbread is similar to thick flour tortillas. It's great for tearing into pieces and dipping in the soup, and it's delicious with yogurt cheese spreads.

1½ cups all-purpose flour

3 tablespoons sesame seeds, toasted (page 38)

½ teaspoon kosher salt

¾ teaspoon sugar

½ teaspoon baking powder

Pinch of baking soda

¼ cup skim milk

¼ cup water

2 tablespoons plain nonfat yogurt

1 tablespoon canola oil

Mix the dry ingredients together in a medium bowl. In a separate bowl, combine the milk, water, yogurt, and oil. Make a well in the center of the dry ingredients and gradually pour in the liquid ones, stirring to make a soft dough. Transfer the dough to a lightly floured surface and knead briefly until smooth. Put the dough in a lightly buttered small bowl. Grease the surface, cover with a damp cloth, and set aside to rest for about 1 hour.

Preheat the oven to 450 degrees. Divide the dough into 4 pieces. Roll out each one on a lightly floured surface until it is no more than ⅛ inch thick and cut it in half. Place the flatbreads on an ungreased baking sheet and bake for 8 to 10 minutes, or until lightly browned. Serve warm.

Makes 8 flatbreads

Steamed Brown Bread

PERHAPS I OWE an apology to the purists out there for my irreverent tinkering, but I could not resist trying to make a version of steamed brown bread that was a cut above the old standby. This is a steamed brown bread with pizzazz! You'll need two 24-ounce cans for steaming the bread.

¾   cup Grand Marnier
½   cup raisins
½   cup coarsely chopped walnuts
1   cup rye flour
1   cup yellow cornmeal
½   cup white bread flour or
      all-purpose flour
½   cup whole wheat flour
2   teaspoons ground cinnamon
1   teaspoon kosher salt
1   teaspoon baking soda
1½ cups nonfat buttermilk
½   cup dark molasses
2   tablespoons grated orange rind

In a small saucepan, heat the Grand Marnier until it simmers. Add the raisins and walnuts. Cover, remove from the heat, and set aside.

Fill a canning kettle or a very large pot with about 6 inches of water. Cover and simmer over low heat.

Combine the dry ingredients in a large bowl. In a separate bowl, beat the buttermilk, molasses, and orange rind. Stir the liquid ingredients into the dry ingredients. Drain the raisin and nut mixture and fold it into the batter.

Spoon the batter into two ungreased 24-ounce cans. Cover tightly with foil and lower the cans into the kettle. The water should come no more than two-thirds of the way up the sides of the cans. Bring the kettle to a boil, cover, and cook the breads for 1 hour, replenishing the water as necessary, until the breads have risen in the cans and spring back to the touch. About 15 minutes before they are ready, preheat the oven to 400 degrees.

Remove the cans from the kettle. Bake for an additional 5 minutes, uncovered, in the oven. Cool the breads in the cans on a wire rack. Gently shake the breads out of the cans, slice, and serve.

Makes 2 loaves

THERE'S NOTHING NEW UNDER THE SUN, so why try to reinvent the wheel? Those are fighting words when tossed in my direction and have the opposite effect of discouraging me. I prefer clichés like "Necessity is the mother of invention" and "Nothing ventured, nothing gained." What do you mean, potato-leek soup has been done? I say, Hang on to your apron and press forward, regardless, if you have ideas for improving a recipe or want to concoct something unusual.

Where there's a will, there's a way, provided you keep in mind that you are engaged in a balancing act. The creative part of cooking may be an art, but cooking is more than alchemy; it's chemistry! Salad dressings are suspensions; leavening agents like yeast produce gas; and mixing buttermilk with baking soda combines an acid with a base. The reduction of soup stock by evaporation and melting a solid dollop of butter in a skillet are both basic chemical reactions.

Biscuits are a case in point. Biscuit dough can only withstand so much tweaking because of the almighty forces governing food chemistry. But when it comes to biscuit *size*, it's liberty hall! It occurred to me that if a recipe for biscuits would serve four people, assuming everyone would eat at least three biscuits (or would like to), instead of cutting out many little biscuits, why not cut to the chase? How about fewer larger biscuits, each one four inches wide? They were an instant hit with my dinner guests, who appreciated the convenience of having a decent quantity of biscuits all in one go.

Furthermore, I discovered that by making large biscuits, I did not work the dough very much, and my big biscuits were light and tender. When you are committed to getting at least a dozen biscuits out of a recipe, you often have to recycle the scraps of dough from the cutting operation, gathering them together and rolling them out several times, exciting the gluten in the flour. The goal is to distribute the particles of fat evenly throughout the flour, stick it together with liquid, and roll out the dough with a minimum of kneading to keep that gluten under control. If you handle the dough too much, you can end up with some pretty tough customers in the biscuit department.

I have found these sorts of culinary chemical revelations helpful, being the type of cook who appreciates understanding how and why things succeed or fail in my kitchen. Knowledge is power, and faced with uncharted waters (or biscuits), every little bit helps.

Big Buttermilk Biscuits

Serve these big and tender biscuits hot from the oven and watch them disappear. You will need a circular cookie cutter 4 inches in diameter. Serve with Lemon Honey Butter (page 245).

---

2 cups all-purpose flour
1 tablespoon baking powder
½ teaspoon kosher salt
¼ cup canola oil
1 cup nonfat buttermilk

Preheat the oven to 450 degrees. Lightly oil a baking sheet with vegetable spray and set aside.

In a large bowl, combine the flour, baking powder, and salt. Drizzle the oil over the mixture and blend it in with your fingers. Add the buttermilk, stirring to form a stiff dough. Use a little additional flour, if necessary, to prevent the dough from sticking.

On a lightly floured surface, roll the dough out so that it is large enough to be cut into 8 biscuits. Cut out the biscuits and place them on the baking sheet. Bake for 12 minutes and serve hot from the oven.

Makes 8 biscuits

Spreads

THERE ARE SOME PERKS TO BEING A CHILD, NOT the least of which is being the recipient of goodies from the kitchens of indulgent grown-ups. It didn't take long for me to figure out what the rewards would be for accompanying my mother when she visited her various friends. If there was only one cookie to be had at the end of an

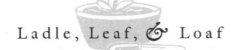

interminable afternoon sitting on the couch and sticking to the plastic upholstery covers at Mrs. Kazaks's house, I made myself scarce if my mother was headed in that direction. But if she was going to visit her Swedish friend, I was in the car before anyone else, because at Dora Harrison's house, I got thick slices of fresh homemade bread with butter and brown sugar. I can't say that as a child I developed any Pavlovian association between good behavior and a slice of fresh bread with a delectable spread—I was a little too feral for that—but I did learn there were a lot of interesting things to put on bread besides peanut butter.

Those bread, butter, and brown sugar treats of long ago were also my first introduction to open-faced sandwiches. It was an entirely new concept that in my mind hovered somewhere between fancy food for teatime and what grown-ups ate at cocktail parties. That is, until I went to college and ate bread with hummus and, as the saying goes, got real. The open-faced sandwich suddenly shed its bourgeois pretensions and became honest fare. And that's where it has remained for me, the perfect complement to a bowl of soup and a plate of salad.

Lemon Honey Butter

LEMON HONEY BUTTER is heavenly melting on hot popovers and biscuits.

---

6 tablespoons butter, at room
   temperature

1 tablespoon honey

½ teaspoon grated lemon rind,
   plus extra for sprinkling

In a small food processor, combine the butter with the honey and lemon rind. Blend well. Transfer to a small bowl. Decorate with a sprinkling of the grated lemon rind. Cover and chill thoroughly before serving.

Makes about ½ cup

Green Onion Butter

HOT STUFF! A scallion and cilantro takeover, with a taste of cumin for a nice background flavor. This spread is excellent served with corn breads and Seeded Soda Bread (page 227).

6 tablespoons butter, at room
　temperature
1 small scallion, thinly sliced, plus
　a few thin slices for garnish
1 tablespoon fresh cilantro
　leaves, plus 1 leaf
　for garnish
　Pinch of cumin

In a small food processor, combine the butter, scallion, cilantro, and cumin. Blend well. Force the mixture through a sieve, using a rubber spatula. Transfer to a small bowl. Press the cilantro leaf on top, and sprinkle with a few thin slices of the scallion. Cover and chill thoroughly before serving.

Makes about ½ cup

Chive Butter

THIS RECIPE gives chives a chance to shine as the featured ingredient, with a supporting cast of spicy green peppercorns and the essence of lemon.

---

6 tablespoons butter, at room
   temperature

2½ tablespoons minced fresh chives

⅛ teaspoon grated lemon rind

⅛ teaspoon crushed green peppercorns

1 chive flower or minced fresh chives
   for garnish

In a small food processor, combine the butter, chives, lemon rind, and peppercorns. Blend well. Force the mixture through a sieve, using a rubber spatula. Transfer to a small bowl and press the chive flower on top or sprinkle with the minced chives. Cover and chill thoroughly before serving.

Makes about ½ cup

Tarragon Butter

FRESH TARRAGON is the aristocrat of green herbs. Blended with butter and a hint of pepper, it makes an elegant spread for French Bread (page 198) and for Saffron Rolls (page 191).

---

2 tablespoons fresh tarragon leaves, plus 1 leaf for garnish

6 tablespoons butter, at room temperature

¼ teaspoon crushed green peppercorns

In a small food processor, chop the tarragon. Add the softened butter and crushed peppercorns. Blend well. Force the mixture through a sieve, using a rubber spatula. Transfer to a small bowl and garnish with the tarragon leaf. Cover and chill thoroughly before serving.

Makes about ½ cup

Cilantro and Jalapeño Butter

THIS SPICY BUTTER goes well with the flavors of corn bread, soda bread, and biscuits.

2 tablespoons minced pickled
  jalapeño peppers
2 tablespoons fresh cilantro leaves,
  plus 1 leaf for garnish
1 garlic clove, chopped
6 tablespoons unsalted butter,
  at room temperature
1 teaspoon brine from the peppers

In a small food processor, chop the peppers, cilantro leaves, and garlic. Add the softened butter and pepper liquid and blend well. Force the mixture through a sieve, using a rubber spatula. Transfer to a small bowl and garnish with the cilantro leaf. Cover and chill thoroughly before serving.

Makes about ½ cup

Anchovy Butter

THIS CONDIMENT will satisfy the anchovy lovers and quite possibly lure anchovy-resistant diners into our camp. Serve with Crusty Whole Wheat Bread (page 199).

3 ounces anchovy fillets, drained

6 tablespoons unsalted butter, at room temperature

½ teaspoon crushed pink peppercorns

Chopped fresh chives for garnish

Pulverize the anchovies in a small food processor. Add the softened butter and crushed pink peppercorns. Blend well. Force the mixture through a sieve, using a rubber spatula. Transfer to a small bowl and garnish with a sprinkling of fresh chives. Cover and chill thoroughly before serving.

Makes about ½ cup

Lemon Garlic Neufchâtel Spread

Each of the ingredients in this recipe, mixed with Neufchâtel cheese, would be tasty, but put them all together, and the whole is greater than the sum of its parts. This spread goes well with Seeded Soda Bread (page 227).

6 ounces Neufchâtel cheese,
   at room temperature

¼ teaspoon grated lemon rind,
   plus extra for garnish

1 tablespoon freshly squeezed
   and strained lemon juice

1 large garlic clove, pressed
   Freshly ground black pepper

Combine the ingredients in a small food processor and blend well. Transfer to a small bowl and garnish with a sprinkling of the grated lemon rind. Cover and chill thoroughly before serving.

Makes about ½ cup

Sun-Dried Tomato Tapenade

IN THIS UNUSUAL collaboration of high-profile flavors and textures,
the ingredients make culinary music together.

⅓ cup sun-dried tomatoes

½ cup pitted kalamata olives

½ cup walnut pieces

2 ounces Neufchâtel cheese,
  at room temperature

1 tablespoon small capers

Pour boiling water over the tomatoes in a small bowl. Set aside to soak until softened, about 10 minutes. Drain.

In a small food processor or blender, combine the tomatoes, olives, and walnuts. Pulse until the ingredients are coarsely chopped. Add the Neufchâtel cheese and blend the ingredients together briefly; the mixture should still be textured. Transfer to a small bowl and garnish with the capers. The spread can be served chilled or at room temperature.

Makes about ¾ cup

Parmesan Cheese Spread

PARMESAN CHEESE is like the party guest who gets along well with just about everyone, no matter what the seating chart. This spread tastes great with all kinds of breads—try it with Savory Zucchini Bread (page 233), Potato-Onion Rye Bread (page 202), and Pine Nut Breadsticks (page 190), to name a few.

---

4 ounces Neufchâtel cheese, at room
    temperature
¼ cup freshly grated Parmesan cheese
⅛ teaspoon crushed green peppercorns
1 tablespoon parsley leaves, plus
    1 leaf for garnish

Combine the ingredients in a small food processor. Pulse until the ingredients are thoroughly blended. Transfer to a small bowl and garnish with the parsley leaf. The spread can be served chilled or at room temperature.

Makes about ½ cup

Pesto Cheese Spread

THIS IS SINFUL, it tastes so good. Serve with Forty-Clove Garlic Bread (page 196), Onion Flatbread (page 212), or Sesame Flatbread (page 238).

½ cup firmly packed fresh basil leaves

½ cup pecans, plus 1 pecan half
   for garnish

¼ cup freshly grated Parmesan cheese

2 small garlic cloves, pressed

6 ounces Neufchâtel cheese,
   at room temperature

In a small food processor, chop the basil with the pecans. Transfer the mixture to a small bowl. Stir in the Parmesan cheese and garlic. Using a large fork or a thin rubber spatula, blend in the Neufchâtel cheese. Mix the ingredients thoroughly. Transfer to a small, decorative bowl and garnish with the pecan half. The spread can be served chilled or at room temperature.

Makes about 1¼ cups

Goat Cheese and Sweet Red Pepper Spread

WHEN I WAS raising goats and making cheese, I was always testing new ways to add interesting flavors to my cheese products. One day I mixed some pickled sweet red peppers into the fresh cheese and drizzled it with oil. It was dynamite. This recipe reminds me of the dining pleasures of my cheese-making days. Serve with Onion Flatbread (page 212), Olive Bread (page 214), or French Bread (page 198).

½ teaspoon olive oil

2 teaspoons minced red bell pepper

¼ teaspoon crushed pink peppercorns

6 ounces fresh chèvre, crumbled

   Kosher salt to taste

1 leaf flat-leaf parsley

Heat the oil in a small skillet over medium heat. Cook the pepper until it softens, 3 to 5 minutes. In a small food processor or blender, combine the red pepper, peppercorns, chèvre, and salt. Pulse until the ingredients are thoroughly blended. Adjust the seasoning. Transfer to a small bowl and garnish with the parsley leaf. Cover and chill thoroughly before serving.

Makes about ⅔ cup

Roasted Garlic Yogurt Cheese

ONLY BREADS with a strong character need apply . . .
This spread of thick, creamy yogurt cheese blended with a shameless amount
of roasted garlic is delicious with Pita Breads (page 194) or Olive Bread (page 214).

1 cup Plain Yogurt Cheese (page 41)

5 large roasted garlic cloves (page 196)

⅛ teaspoon kosher salt

  Pinch of paprika

Combine the ingredients in a small food processor and blend thoroughly. To enhance the flavors, refrigerate for at least 1 hour before serving.

Makes 1 cup

Ladle, Leaf, & Loaf

Green Peppercorn Yogurt Cheese

Tangy and peppery, this can be used as a spread
or as a condiment for soups.

---

1 cup Plain Yogurt Cheese (page 41)
½ teaspoon crushed green peppercorns
1 small garlic clove, pressed
  Kosher salt to taste

In a small bowl, stir together the yogurt cheese, peppercorns, garlic, and salt. Mix well. To enhance the flavors, refrigerate for at least 1 hour before serving.

Makes about 1 cup

Eggplant Spread

WALNUTS ADD TEXTURE and flavor to this classic eggplant spread.
Because of their shared Mediterranean roots, it is a natural choice to serve with
Pita Breads (page 194) and Sesame Flatbread (page 238).

1   medium eggplant (about 1¼ pounds)

½   cup walnuts

⅓   cup chopped fresh parsley leaves

¼   cup tahini

2   garlic cloves

1   tablespoon freshly squeezed and
    strained lemon juice

½   teaspoon kosher salt
    Freshly ground black pepper

Preheat the oven to 400 degrees. Pierce the eggplant once with a fork, to allow steam to escape while it bakes, and cut off the stem. Place the eggplant on a piece of foil and bake until it is tender, about 1 hour. Remove from the oven and cool slightly. Cut in half and scrape the flesh from the skin.

Puree the eggplant in a food processor. Add the remaining ingredients, one at a time, as the food processor is running. Transfer to a small bowl and chill thoroughly before serving.

Makes about 2 cups

Tahini Honey Spread

TAHINI AND HONEY blended together make an unusual spread that is both sweet and rich with the flavor of sesame seeds. Serve with Pumpkin Bread (page 210) or Whole Wheat Soda Bread (page 229).

¼ cup tahini (available in health food stores and some supermarkets)

¼ cup honey

⅛ teaspoon ground coriander

⅛ teaspoon ground cinnamon

⅛ teaspoon grated lemon rind, plus extra for garnish

In a small bowl, mix together the tahini and honey. Add the remaining ingredients. Blend thoroughly. Transfer to a small serving bowl and garnish with a sprinkling of the grated lemon rind. Serve at room temperature.

Makes about ½ cup

Hazelnut Butter

HAZELNUTS AND SWEETNESS are inseparable and make a perfectly alluring combination.
Try Hazelnut Butter with Cardamom Raisin Bread (page 207),
Anise Bread (page 195), or Pumpkin Bread (page 210).

½ cup toasted hazelnuts (page 38),
    plus 1 toasted hazelnut for garnish

½ teaspoon ground cinnamon

1½ teaspoons honey

2 tablespoons butter, at room
    temperature

Combine the nuts and cinnamon in a small food processor. Pulse until the nuts are finely ground. Add the honey and butter and pulse until thoroughly blended. Transfer to a small bowl and garnish with the hazelnut. Cover and refrigerate before serving.

Makes about ⅔ cup

Ladle, Leaf, & Loaf

Almond Neufchâtel Spread

THIS RICH, almond-flavored spread is meant for the sweet side of the quick bread family.

---

6 ounces Neufchâtel cheese,
   at room temperature

¼ cup toasted almonds (page 38),
   finely ground, plus 1 almond
   for garnish

2 teaspoons honey

¼ teaspoon freshly ground black pepper

2 drops pure almond extract

Combine all the ingredients in a small food processor. Pulse until the ingredients are thoroughly blended. Transfer to a small bowl and garnish with the almond. The spread can be served chilled or at room temperature.

Makes about ½ cup

Ladle, Leaf, & Loaf

Walnut Neufchâtel Spread

A SWEET LITTLE CONCOCTION to serve with Steamed Brown Bread (page 239), Pumpkin Bread (page 210), or Anadama Bread (page 208).

---

6 ounces Neufchâtel cheese, at room temperature

¼ cup toasted walnuts (page 38), finely chopped, plus 1 toasted walnut half for garnish

2 teaspoons honey

1 teaspoon orange juice concentrate
 Grated rind of 1 orange

Mix all the ingredients together in a small food processor. Pulse until the ingredients are thoroughly blended. Transfer to a small serving bowl and garnish with the toasted walnut half. Cover and chill thoroughly before serving.

Makes about 1 cup

Ladle, Leaf, & Loaf

Index

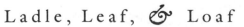

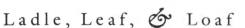